Conscious Food

Sustainable Growing, Spiritual Eating

by the same author

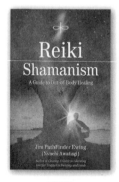
ISBN
978-1-84409-133-1

ISBN
978-1-84409-082-2

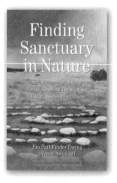
ISBN
978-1-84409-095-2

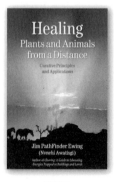
ISBN
978-1-84409-111-9

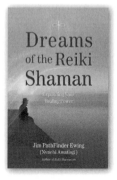
ISBN
978-1-84409-568-1

available from your local bookstore
or directly from www.findhornpress.com

Conscious Food
Sustainable Growing, Spiritual Eating

Jim PathFinder Ewing
(Nvnehi Awatisgi)

FINDHORN PRESS

© Jim PathFinder Ewing 2012

The right of Jim PathFinder Ewing to be identified as the
author of this work has been asserted by him in accordance
with the Copyright, Designs and Patents Act 1998.

Published in 2012 by Findhorn Press, Scotland

ISBN 978-1-84409-596-4

A CIP record for this title is available from the British Library.

Edited by Nicky Leach
Cover and Interior design by Damian Keenan
Printed and bound in the US

1 2 3 4 5 6 7 8 9 17 16 15 14 13 12

Published by
Findhorn Press
117-121 High Street,
Forres IV36 1AB,
Scotland, UK

t +44 (0)1309 690582
f +44 (0)131 777 2711
e info@findhornpress.com
www.findhornpress.com

*Creator bestows so many gifts
upon the world.*

*How wonderful that we are able to give
thanks in return!*

In our times, there are matters of Spirit and matters of worldly things.

But where do worldly things come from, if not from Spirit?

Let us allow Spirit and matter to be united in our consciousness, and see the wholeness of life.

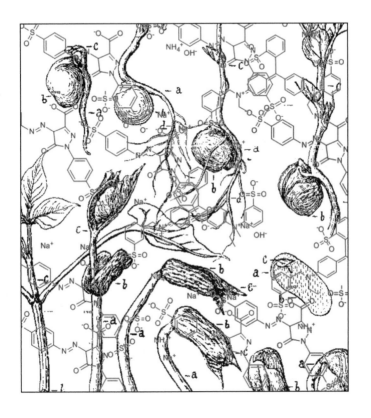

Contents

Giving Thanks!

I am most indebted to the many colleagues, teachers, and organizations that have helped me be able to offer insights and understandings. As in previous books, I am thankful for my indigenous teachers, who taught me fundamental ways of looking at the world, to see with my "Spirit eyes," along with continued instruction into later life.

I am grateful for the members and officers of various nonprofits over the past 30 years, who have allowed me to serve as a volunteer in executive capacities. With regard to the subject matter of this book, I am particularly grateful for the work I have been able to do with the whole foods and organic grocery business, and organizations concentrating on wildlife, ecology, agriculture, conservation, and sustainability issues. They include the Mississippi Wildlife Federation, for which I was honored to serve as editor of its magazine for several years, a role that allowed me to learn about conservation issues and the various public interest groups involved in the environmental movement; Ducks Unlimited, which, during the time I served on its state board and as editor of its publications for six years, allowed me to learn the ins and outs of congressional Farm Bills for managing agricultural acreages and wetlands; Rainbow Natural Grocery Cooperative, where I served as vice president for the board of directors and on the executive committee, learning the hard lessons of running a million-dollar-a-year organic grocery business; Gaining Ground – Sustainability Institute of Mississippi, a statewide educational outreach nonprofit, focused on improving poverty, education, agriculture, health, and the environment, where I served on the board of directors; the Mississippi Urban Forest Council, where I served on the board of directors helping to make cities "green" and promoting "edible" forests; and the Mississippi Fruit & Vegetable Growers Association, the state's small farm trade organization, where I served as president. My experiences with these three latter organizations taught me important lessons about the vital issues of growers and the academic disciplines and current issues of today's food scene. In addition, my current service on the board of Certified Naturally Grown, the grassroots alternative to certified organic for small farmers, ranchers, and beekeepers, has given me an understanding of direct marketing in agriculture at the national level, for which I am grateful.

I owe a huge debt of gratitude to Ronnie Agnew, former executive editor of *The Clarion-Ledger* in Jackson, Mississippi, and now executive director of Mississippi Public Broadcasting, for encouraging me to write a weekly column on organic food, farming, and gardening. The column developed a large and enthusiastic following and allowed me to test my ideas and learn from the experts—the readers and farmers, eaters and gardeners across the state of Mississippi and, through the Internet, the world. Throughout, I am grateful for my 35-plus years as a journalist for newspapers in Tennessee and Mississippi, covering all aspects of news and farming, ranching and dairying, and people, places, and things, and learning how to turn objective reality "out there" into words in print.

I'm grateful for the hundreds of students and clients I've worked with over the years, who have taught me so much about energy medicine, the mind, and the heart, as well as the readers of my books, who encourage me to continue writing by freely offering me their gratitude, interest, and support.

My list of acknowledgments wouldn't be complete without a nod to my late father, James Ewing, who grew up on a farm himself, the product of generations of farmers in America since 1734, and before that for untold generations in Scotland. He taught me to feel, smell, and taste soil to determine its pH and quality—a type of soil testing that is as enduring as people living intimately with the earth.

I wish to offer gratitude also to my mother, Alice Ewing, under whose watchful gaze I, as a boy, spent endless hours digging, pruning, and tending her prize-winning rose bushes. Among many lessons, I learned that one's goals are not won without labor—and perhaps, a few drops of blood and tears from hidden thorns along the way.

And, of course, I'm most indebted to my wife, Annette, who serves as my editor, companion, and friend. Too often, she does the lion's share of work in our little ShooFly Farm, happily toiling in the hot sun while I sit in the air-conditioned indoors writing these books!

In all ways, she is truly a blessing in my life, and I'm grateful to be on this Earth walk beside her.

Preface

In your hands is the sixth book in the PathFinder series. These books deal with concepts variously called spiritual ecology, eco-spirituality, and environmental shamanism; together, they introduce a series of tools that can help us reconnect to our natural selves.

Each of the first five books explores different facets of a way of healing, health, and wholeness and their applications to daily life.

The first three books constitute a trilogy of "people, places, and things" in the shamanic way of viewing the world and all beings. The fourth book, *Reiki Shamanism: A Guide to Out of Body Healing*, combines Reiki with shamanism, and the fifth book, *Dreams of the Reiki Shaman: Expanding Your Healing Power*, builds upon that foundation and incorporates student input and personal experience in the perception of nonordinary reality, not limited to the shamanic journey.

This book expands on that body of knowledge by focusing on a critical aspect of our lives: the growing and eating of food. We will revisit ancient concepts of Spirit and their relationship to the underpinnings of the Western food paradigm and explore them with modern understandings and perspectives. This evolution of food consciousness, at this critical turning point, can work wonders in the world, not only for ourselves at the individual level but also globally.

This book can be enjoyed as a stand-alone text or as a natural follow-on from the previous books. Practitioners of energy medicine and general readers alike will find that the information in this book will help you expand your horizons and reveal new pathways to personal growth and development. It is my hope that this will help lead you toward greater nourishment, healing, health, and wholeness—for yourself and for the community of Earth.

If you have picked up this book, doubtless you are aware of the impact that food production has had on Earth and its communities. It has become increasingly obvious that "modern," or so-called "conventional," agriculture is a 70-year-old experiment that has succeeded in many ways but failed miserably as a sustainable practice. There are other ways of sustainably feeding the world's increasing populations—ways that simultaneously build on methods that have worked while rejecting those that lead to an increase in problems. This postmodern way of looking at food production includes a holistic, balanced approach toward those who produce it, as well as what is produced. It requires that we change the way we look at food, spiritually, and the way that we look at each other.

Inevitably, you will find some overlap with areas of the other books. Where other of my books expand more fully on a concept, I have provided a cross-reference to the book or books in question. In that way, if you are interested in exploring the subject further, you can do some additional reading.

On the Structure of the Book

This book is divided into three chapters:

- The first chapter explores how we have lost sight of the most basic connection we have with the land—our food—which today has somehow become disconnected from Spirit. For thousands of years, from prehistoric times to early Christians and Native American societies, agrarian societies lived according to certain bedrock values. Among these was respect for women, a value that allowed the Divine to be recognized in everyday life, including acceptance of angels and other ethereal beings and a close association between food and Spirit. By simply seeing food and the growing of it as a spiritual practice, as most recently promulgated by anthroposophist Rudolf Steiner in the early 20th century, we can begin to see humanity in its wholeness.

- The second chapter explores new scientific discoveries in the world of agriculture that offer a modern understanding of what once were, in early agrarian times, matters of mere superstition, or belief without understanding. I examine how the hidden world of Spirit has never left—although, in many instances, it has been slumbering, and is only now beginning to be measured and understood by modern science. I show how this postmodern way of doing things, which incorporates ideas from both the past and the future, views the making of food as subject to change—and with it, not only our perceptions of our world but ways to live in it.

- The third chapter provides practical tools for ways we can change the way we participate in the world of food production, from the smallest actions to overriding beliefs, through the concept of negative entropy (syntropy) and practicing mindful biocultural behavior. This practical, spiritual way of living, as outlined, is actually the way of the ancestors, but on a global scale that can truly effect massive and lasting change. This marriage of Spirit and an emerging global consciousness with regard to food production in local communities offers the chance for a second revolution, following the discovery of agriculture 10,000 years ago. Our food choices can remake agriculture in healthful and sustainable ways, while simultaneously remaking ourselves and our world.

At the end of each chapter, you'll find *Jim's Notebook* entries about growing your own food, or joining others to do so. These tips may be suitable for temperate climates, based as they are in the American South specifically, but more generally aimed at areas of moderate rainfall and temperatures. (Those who live in the American Southwest, for example, would have to use more drought-sensitive techniques and plant varieties.) As with my previous books, I have included key words that may be searched on the Internet to allow you to further explore and improve your understanding of a topic. The appendix includes a list of resources available on Twitter, smartphone apps, or for use on your personal computer. All of my books are currently available in electronic format.

At the back of the book, you will find a glossary of terms specific to the topics covered in the book, as well as an extensive bibliography covering a reading list of publications that I believe help us understand the new ways in which food and agriculture are perceived in today's world.

Our website, Healing the Earth/Ourselves, at *www.blueskywaters.com*, offers books, CDs, tools, and additional reading material—including Reiki, shamanism, energy medicine, organics, ecology, environment, farming, and food—that may be ordered online, as well as information about periodic classes and workshops and access to our monthly newsletter.

This book is by no means definitive on the subjects of cultural anthropology, energy medicine, or agricultural sciences. In this book, my intention is to offer a look at various spiritual facets of the world and of growing food. These are based on my own experiences, and are intended as a gateway for you, the reader, to begin to engage with the concepts. My way of doing things is not the only way; there are infinite paths to insight through Spiritlands. The purpose of all of my books is to help provide an opening for you to discern your own truth, and ultimately find your own path.

As in previous books, I define "healing" as the ability to find wholeness and balance within, the way that it was taught to me, not through being cured by Western allopathic medicine. Equally, I define "medicine" as the intrinsic power within a thing to be whole. Nothing in this book, or in my previous books, should be construed as offering medical advice.

My intention in writing this book is that it serves as a guide for you. I hope it will be instrumental in changing the way you perceive the world and help foster an appreciation of some of life's greatest pleasures: growing and eating food. May you find many blessings on this path!

Returning Spirit to Our Food

Where do clouds come from?
They come from the eye that perceives them.

— *PATHWAYS* [1]

One of my teachers, a Lakota medicine man who was taught Spiritways from childhood, told me several years ago that when he was a boy, there often was no food for his family to eat. His father, a medicine man, would then have them sit at an empty table and they would eat Spirit Food. He showed me how they would perceive the food, the table, the taste of each fruit or vegetable, their bodies being filled with food, and the nourishment they received. "You wouldn't get fat on it," he laughed, "but it kept you alive."

Over the course of a couple of years, I had occasion to practice his teaching on fasts and vision quests. In time, I learned that such a skill is not confined to Native American medicine people; it is a well-known practice among some shamans and eastern mystics, and stems from ancient Hindu and Buddhist teachings. It requires an intimate understanding of one's spiritual and physical body, essentially living sustainably upon the Ki (*chee*), or life-force energy, of the earth by being impeccable in its use.

For example, if you maintain a high level of energy, or vibration rate—by focusing on acceptance and gratitude for all the bounteous gifts of Earth—you can exist for many days eating "Spirit Food." Of course, we all have to live in the physical world. Our spirits may be of Sky and Creator, but our bodies are of Earth.

When we lack balance in our diet, we feel it in many ways. In the past century or so, too many of us have lost the Spirit part of our physical food. Even saying "grace," or blessing our food, has fallen out of fashion, or lost its original form or meaning. In olden times, because food was often not fresh, people held hands over it to raise its vibration rate through prayer, as a method of cleansing it. This spiritual blessing of food wasn't a rote act or formality; it was considered an essential safeguard to health.

We also seem to have lost our connection to the spirituality of the land, which goes hand in hand with the basic connection to our natural selves. Instead of a gift of Spirit and Earth, sown with heart and hand, to nourish and sustain, our modern agriculture has lost its moorings; it is adrift in the meetingplace of technology and a marketplace with increasingly short-sighted, topsy-turvy values.

With each seed we can reclaim it, planting our hopes, dreams, and intentions for abundance, and infusing our produce with gratitude toward Creator. Let us return to Spirit Food. Not the insubstantial kind that merely keeps us fed but, through the marriage of Heaven and Earth, real food that is grown with respect for the interconnectedness of all things.

Let us begin this journey of returning Spirit to our food!

CHAPTER ONE

Edible Prayers

A Brief, Selective History of Food
and Spirit in the Western World

*There's nothing fundamentally wrong with people.
Given a story to enact that puts them in accord with
the world, they will live in accord with the world.
But given a story to enact that puts them at odds with
the world, as yours does, they will live at odds with
the world. Given a story to enact in which they are
the lords of the world, they will act as the lords of the
world. And, given a story to enact in which the world
is a foe to be conquered, they will conquer it like a
foe, and one day, inevitably, their foe will lie bleeding
to death at their feet, as the world is now.*

—*DANIEL QUINN, ISHMAEL: AN ADVENTURE
OF THE MIND AND SPIRIT*

Who speaks for Spirit in our food? Today, a growing number of people are beginning to revisit the connection between food and Spirit. It is one of the oldest concepts in human history. To get an inkling of our connection, and what has been lost, we must go back in time—first a little, then a lot.

The most modern voices for Spirit in food are those who practice biodynamic farming, a system developed in the early 20th century by scientist and philosopher Rudolf Steiner which he called The Agriculture Course.

Steiner developed The Agriculture Course because he was concerned about the growing impact of synthetic chemicals on agriculture and saw it as a threat not only to human nutrition but to Earth itself. The course is a series of lectures which, at the invitation of Count Carl Keyserlinck, Steiner gave in 1924 to an assembly of 130 farmers in Eastern Germany who had noticed a lack of vitality in their crops. [1]

These lectures caused a sensation and launched the biodynamic farming movement—a movement that has continued to this day but has never achieved mainstream status, despite a resurgence of interest in recent years.

Prior to The Agriculture Course, Steiner had earned his reputation as the leading scientist and philosopher of his time as editor of the scientific works of Johann Wolfgang von Goethe. But after developing The Agriculture Course and exploring esoteric matters, Steiner found his following among mainstream scientists fading. He called his research "spiritual science," or Anthroposophy (Greek *anthropos*, or "human being," and *sophia*, "wisdom"), an offshoot of the scientific method expounded by Descartes. It was dismissed by the scientific community, however, before it could receive adequate scrutiny and be developed in a meaningful way.

Steiner's intention was to draw the public's attention to the negative direction that agricultural science was headed—namely, a growing reliance on a reductionist approach to supplying plant needs, using NPK (nitrogen, phosphorus, and potash) without the trace elements that provide health. But without the backing of scientific colleagues, Steiner found his ideas marginalized. Their survival is largely due to a small number of farmers and Steiner's following in the Theosophical Society, founded by Madame Blavatsky, who continue to practice biodynamic agriculture.

In his book, *What is Biodynamics? A Way to Heal and Revitalize the Earth*, Steiner defined biodynamic agriculture thus:

- Earth itself is a living being that is being killed by human practices, not the least of which is increasing reliance on synthetic chemicals needed to support monoculture growing systems.
- Humanity is not able to evolve spiritually because it is being fed "dead" food, that is, nutritionally deficient agricultural products as the result of using synthetics in agriculture.
- The unseen, noncorporal forces of Nature are withdrawing their assistance with the growing of food crops because of the use of synthetics and poisons driving them away.
- Crops are no longer being planted in harmony with sun, moon, and other significant astrological alignments, which humankind has relied upon since the birth of agriculture to stay in harmony with the planet and all beings.
- Agriculture is not being approached from a spiritual point of view.

Some of these concerns sound like very modern ideas; indeed, they would be at home in the practice of any of a dozen energy medicine modalities, and among many farmers themselves.

Some of Steiner's ideas have flourished. Readers may be familiar with the Waldorf schools based on Steiner's philosophies, which incorporate a humanistic approach to pedagogy. As of 2012, there were 1,025 independent Waldorf schools around the globe. The approach emphasizes the appreciation of imagination in learning and fosters ever increasing levels of sophistication, regardless of the student's age.

Many people find Steiner's approach to farming off-putting because he states his ideas in archaic language, using concepts that originated with the late 19th- and early 20th-century notions of "the ethers." Steiner's understanding of noncorporal beings stems from ancient Hindu writings, explained in his lecture on Elementals on

November 3, 1923, as being "those from the Indian Brahma, Vishnu, and Shiva," which refer to undines, fire salamanders, and gnomes. His practical agricultural applications stem from 17th-century European peasant practices, which not only are now mostly forgotten but were rather limited in appeal when he spoke about them in the early part of the 20th century.

Today, energy medicine and spiritual ways of viewing the world have gone mainstream, as more people experience a variety of healing and spiritual modalities. For example, the cultivation of life force that Steiner believed was essential to healing the earth is at the heart of Reiki, a healing modality from Japan that millions of people around the globe now use. (The name is derived from the Japanese: *Rei*, or "guided," and *ki,* "life force energy," also known as qi, or chi.) In other words, those who practice energy medicine techniques and understandings to grow food are directly accessing the energy Steiner sought to nurture; they just use other names and concepts.

I practice what I call Reiki Shamanism, which combines visioning through the shamanic journey with the healing modality of Reiki. The practitioner uses a drum to achieve a dreamlike state, caused by the steady beat stimulating theta waves in the brain. Once that mental state is reached, one can direct visioning to perceive reality in unique ways, and apply Reiki healing where needed. By thus broadening perception of reality without the use of any drug, the Reiki Shaman is able to perceive the forces that were considered flights of fancy a century ago. Another name for it is "visualized prayer."

It is my contention that by applying energy modalities to the art of growing food, modern people can build upon Steiner's vision, and raise the vibration level of Earth. This could well be a path to a new, efficient, and beneficial way of producing food, exceeding any expectation he might have had in his time and place. With millions of people around the globe now learning and practicing techniques such as Reiki, shamanism, tai chi, yoga, and other methods that transcend the body to bring harmony to themselves and their surroundings, a profound change in the way we view what we put into our bodies can have lasting effects upon Earth and our societies.

But to get where we need to go, we must look deeper into history and uncover the ancient ways of growing food with Spirit that have been obscured by time. These ancient practices have something to offer us in terms of a different perspective on how we might approach growing food today. In making way for the new, sometimes something essential is swept away, and this may be to our detriment.

Food, God, and Soil: The Basics
for Europeans in the Americas

A crucial feature of daily life from the earliest days of American settlement all the way to the mid-1900s was the belief in God, or Providence, a Higher Power, or Divine appointees as an essential partner in helping to provide food for the table. Puritan immigrants from Great Britain, some of the first Europeans on North American soil, may have been certain that an angry God ruled over them, but they also knew that what they provided with the sweat of their brows was in partnership with a Divine deity. Both were of equal importance in ensuring a good harvest ("Moreover the profit of the earth is for all: the king himself is served by the field"-- Ecclesiastes 5:9).

Things began to shift in the decades following the Louisiana Purchase in 1803, as American politicians extolled the virtues of an empire and of unbridled technological progress characterized by the expansion of the railroads out West, until the Civil War, and resuming thereafter. Philosophers, however, were concerned that Civilization would tilt the balance away from Nature. Among them was Henry David Thoreau, one of the founding members (along with Ralph

Waldo Emerson) of the Transcendantalists, a group of Romantics who extolled the virtues of Nature in human healing. Indeed, in *The Maine Woods*, Thoreau freely admitted that he felt more comfortable working in his bean patch than in carrying out other pursuits. In *Walking*, he asserted: "In short, all good things are wild and free."

Sustainability, as it would be called today, was a guiding belief among the Transcendalists. "Nothing in Nature is exhausted in its first use," wrote Ralph Waldo Emerson in 1849. "When a thing has served an end to the uttermost, it is wholly new for ulterior service. In God, every end is converted to a new means."

The Transcendalists, and many of those who tilled the fields, were followers of a system of agriculture that would now be called organic or eco-farming. And this was nothing new. It had been practiced, in fact, from the outset of American independence, most famously by Thomas Jefferson, principal author of the Declaration of Independence and third president of the United States.

Jefferson collected plants and firmly believed in the use of natural fertilizers as medicine against blight. In 1785, referring to those who practiced natural farming, Jefferson wrote: "Cultivators of the earth are the most valuable citizens. They are the most vigorous, the most independent, the most virtuous, and they are tied to their country and wedded to its liberty and interests by the most lasting bonds."

These may have been new ideas for the first Americans, but they were age-old ideas among the First Americans, the Native people of the Americas. The Native American Iroquois Confederacy heavily influenced the thoughts and writings of Benjamin Franklin, Thomas Jefferson, and James Madison. Iroquois ideas served as the example for Revolutionary America's Albany Plan, the Articles of Confederation and, ultimately, the U.S. Constitution.

Moreover, this pre-Columbian, Native American society also deserves remembering because it offers what today could be the essentials of a sustainable society, embodying social equality, military strength, effective diplomacy, and spiritual power, all based on an agrarian way of life that found Spirit closely allied with the soil. This early democracy existed to help create balance and harmony among their six nations, their neighbors, and the land upon which they all depended.

The modern Iroquois elder, Oren Lyons, has pointed out an important fact, though: The founding fathers expanded upon many of the Six Nations tenets but left out the spiritual aspects, favoring instead the separation of church and state, perhaps to the detriment of the United States. (Also of note: In Iroquois tradition, there would have been Founding Mothers, as the Clan Mothers were the decision-makers in these matrilineal tribes.) [2] Spirit-based, matrilineal Native American societies weren't limited to the northeastern United States, but dominated the entire eastern half of the country and extended into the American Southwest, including the Hopi and Navajo, and up into the northwest to the Arctic Circle with the Tlingit.

Food, God, Soil. The moral connection was so fundamental it was unquestioned in early America. "Those who labor in the earth are the chosen people of God," Thomas Jefferson famously said. It had been embodied in the lifestyles of the First Peoples for many centuries and embedded in their nurturing of crops. By the time Europeans set foot on the Americas, Native Americans had domesticated up to 5,000 different species of food plants, and included species that now constitute up to 60 percent of all crops in cultivation worldwide. Their spiritual ceremonies were closely tied to the seasons, and were characterized by appreciation and gratitude for a benevolent Creator and to Earth and its spirit messengers, similar to other agrarian societies, as we shall explore.

Importantly, though, these first American settlers were people who were not landed gentry in the Old World. They had rights to nothing, in many cases, not even the fruits of the labor of their own hands. Therefore, for the first American settlers, unlike their Native predecessors, the ability to own land and grow and keep one's own food had added value, as a right of property, not a privilege—wedded to the concepts of life and liberty, as unalienable, God-given rights that the U.S. Government was formed to protect.

Spirit in food. Spirit in soil. Spirit in the daily commerce of American life. These guiding principles are often obscured in the grand sweep of history, which tends to focus on trends, wars, and famous personalities. For early Americans lucky enough to own land and farm it, the sun rising each day on a plot of soil one could call one's own was a gift from God—its fruits, as well as its travails and challenges. All life, goods, and commerce sprang from the farm—and that, for a large segment of the population, *was* life in America for a long time, until the advent of World War II.

Agriculture's Biblical Beginnings: Emerging and Dominating Dualities

Going back much farther, the narrative of man's Divine agricultural connection has its roots in the Biblical story of the expulsion of Adam and Eve from the Garden of Eden. To some extent, the story comes across as harsh, but that may be because of its ancient origins. It was a tale told by the Edomites, descendants of Esau, who lived south of the Dead Sea in the arid desert, where nothing grew without great toil and loss. They looked east to the rich valley of the Euphrates River, the cradle of civilization, and west to the life-giving River Nile. You have to wonder, then, whether if that Biblical chapter had been written by a prince of Ur or a scribe of a pharaoh, it would have been so bitter.

Among other lessons, the story of the Fall of Adam and Eve and their subsequent expulsion from the Garden of Eden offers an enduring instruction in its symbolism: The choice by Adam and Eve to eat the fruit in Paradise can be seen as the moment Man went from instinctual eating to exercising conscious choice, thereafter divorcing humans from the unconscious state of Grace exhibited among animal species. It gave us a choice: to thank, embrace, or allow Spirit in our food choices, looking ahead in gladness, or to choose to live apart in sorrow, suffering in our "sin." [3]

Remnants of old stories and archetypes can often be found among the cultural influences on our food and agriculture. They are worth examining, for the light they can shed on our present attitudes.

Origins of Agriculture and Female Spiritual Power

The seeds leading to the disconnect between today's food and spirituality may have been planted with the invention of agriculture itself. As author Barbara Ehrenreich has observed, when mobile hunting males were supplanted by sedentary female-oriented agriculture, they found something else to do: "They invented war." *The Epic of Gilgamesh* (from the Third Dynasty of Ur, 2,150–2,000 BCE), the oldest known major work of literature, can be seen as an example of an agricultural/warrior society, where men are finding work for themselves.

For most of known human history and prehistory, Spirit has been identified as a feminine power—a power that found its highest expression with the founding and upswing of settled agriculture. The earliest known artifact showing the Divine Great Mother is a figurine of the Venus of Willendorf, carved out of limestone around 25,000 BCE and named for the place in Austria where she was unearthed. The oldest known full-size sculpture of a religious deity is also a female figure: Venus of Laussel, circa 25,000–20,000 BCE, carved into the entrance of a cave in southern France.

Farming started the neolithic revolution about 12,000 years ago in the Middle East, with the domestication of goats and sheep and the discovery that certain grains could be planted and harvested. With a steady food source now available, the global population soared from 1 million—a figure that had been stable for eons—to 100 million.

Agriculture began in the town of Catal Huyuk, on the coast of southern Turkey, with the cultivation of barley, around 8,000 BCE. Catal Huyuk is the oldest known town where farmers and hunter-gatherers are known to have lived side by side during the paleolithic period, coexisting for about 2,000 years. Things shifted around 6,000 BCE, when climate change caused the Middle East to become increasingly arid, and dispossessed people moved to the river valleys, where agriculture became the principle food source.

It's worth noting, perhaps, that at this time, when settled urban river-valley agriculture overtook trade and nomadic lifestyles, Jericho (the oldest known city, dating back to at least 8,300 BCE) ceased to exist. Its walls came tumbling down—not with the blowing of horns so much as with the ascendance of the goddess religions, which flourished in the earliest urban settings as a result of settled agriculture. The connection between Spirit as a feminine power and the development of agriculture cannot be overemphasized.

Indeed, as historian Robert MacElvaine noted in his book, *Eve's Seed: Biology, Sexes, and the Course of History*, "Women invented agriculture." Nomadic peoples hardly touched the earth, but settled societies revolutionized human behavior and deepened the cultural and religious connections with the land. The womb (earth and soil) thus becomes sacred space, from which arises the temple, the sacred place where the safety of society as a cooperative whole is offered up, along with its premier archetypes of home, culture, and civilization.

This change from the nomadic to agrarian lifestyle was not without great impact to the environment; early lessons in sustainability were harsh, as growing demands on the land caused erosion of soil and monocultures failed. Sound familiar? Some of these lessons have come back around.

By 3,000 BCE, the role of the feminine as Divine was preeminent, and respect for living things was a crucial element of Nature—from nurture in the cradle to seedlings in the ground to admiration of the human form in full maturity, without shame or fig leaf. This marriage of humanity and Spirit, based on female divinity in agrarian societies, existed for thousands of years.

The sixth century BCE is often called the Axial Age and represents the height or late stage of the agricultural revolution. It saw a flourishing of religious thought across the southern half of Asia and into southeastern Europe that included Lao-tse, Confucius, the Buddha, major Jewish prophets, and the early Greek philosophers. It was a time in which the marriage of food and Spirit was strong and was under the power of, or at least in partnership with, goddess religions, or the Divine feminine.

But there was trouble in Paradise. With the rise of patriarchal nation-states as a result of the food surplus created by farming, the exalted role of women and the balance between men and women in society began to crumble. By the time of Classical Greece, as described in the writings of Homer and Hesiod in the eighth and ninth centuries BCE, women were increasingly considered to be property and spoils of war. Perhaps as a rejection of female-dominated religion, or for whatever reasons, Greek society turned against women as a breed apart.

In Hesiod's words, "woman, for mortal men [became] an evil thing." Women even came to be called *genes gynaikon*, the "race of women," so that they could be objectified as another species. The universal archetype for an unsubordinated woman came to be known as a "gorgon," or a hideous beast too ugly for mortal men to even look at, and who therefore had to be killed by "a hero" cutting off her head.

Unsurprisingly, what was true below was also true above, and among the heavenly Greek pantheon, male storm gods or thunder gods began to displace goddesses as objects of veneration. These gods represented male power and violence, with war the guiding theme. In Greece, Zeus gave birth to Athena, and Aphrodite (Venus) was relegated to the status of Goddess of Love. In Egypt, Isis, the "Mother of God" and "Oldest of the Old," became known as Venus. In India, the storm god Rudra became known as Shiva (taking precedence over the creator goddess, who became Shiva's wife, Shakti) and is often depicted as a stone phallus. Of course, the great Powers of Earth and Sky can never be replaced by mere renaming; universal archetypes are eternal. But the names do reflect changes in political and economic power and signal shifts in cultural behavior.

If womankind developed agriculture (and civilization and culture) and honored the Divine in her own likeness, men came to see themselves as masters over Nature and women, ruling the nation-states that depended on agriculture and extending their military power to conquer others. Agricultural communities in matriarchal societies saw themselves as part of Nature; patriarchal nation-states that arose from agricultural communities saw themselves as above Nature, dominating and ruling it (her) and becoming "as" god. The spiritual connections that existed among Land, Spirit, and Human weakened, with agriculture becoming a product of human will, not a spiritual collaboration.

I feel that the loss of this cultural connection was the root of the modern era that characterizes our values today. In female-dominated agricultural societies, growing food may be viewed as a mother nursing her child: sustenance is given freely and with love. In the Greco-Roman masculine view of agriculture, food was a politicized commodity, used as a means of leveraging control. Food was, and has become, a way of conquering and subduing nations. The fact that only a handful of corporations in the modern United States control the nation's food distribution system—including seed stocks, which they patent and administer with the government's help to export internationally—only highlights how far-reaching this practice has become.

Victims of Progress: Angels of the Essenes and Biblical Women

Food, agriculture, and spirituality coexisted in a common set of beliefs found in the foundations of Christianity, as well. The discovery of The Dead Sea Scrolls—a series of 13 scrolls, including early Judaic texts and the earliest version of the Old Testament, found by wandering desert nomads in 1947—revealed that if Jesus was not an Essene, he certainly held many of their beliefs.

The Essenes were an agrarian society, and archeological evidence suggests that they lived at Qumran (where the scrolls were found) from 135 BCE to shortly after AD 70. Tracings of their beliefs have appeared in ancient Persia, India, Egypt, Tibet, China, Palestine, and Greece. The Pythagoreans and Stoics followed their teachings, as did the Zarathustrans. Jesus is said to have incorporated their ideas in the Seven Beatitudes of the Sermon on the Mount. Their ideas have been reflected in the Jewish Kabala, and handed down in Freemasonry.

"The Songs of the Sabbath Sacrifice" in scrolls 4Q400–407, 11Q17 (also called the Masada Fragment) outlines the importance of incorporating angels into religious ceremonies and offers effusive praise for these "godlike beings of utter holiness." It outlines seven angelic councils, whose duties include the ordering of the cardinal directions and winds (similar to Cherokee lore, by the *unolis*, or winds or directions) and the growing of crops. Left out of the modern Bible are the various Feast Days mentioned in the scrolls, in which thanks is given for crops. This includes "first fruits" of wheat, cereal, and wine, and gratitude for trees (4Q409). This is very similar to Native American celebrations of first leaves of corn, green corn, and ripe corn.

Lost, too, are the underlying teachings in the scrolls that are translated as "The Secret of the Way Things Are." Among the tenets of these early teachings are the exhortation to follow astrology, for its connections with angels—that is, the "host of heaven" communicates through astrology (4Q416), and that the angels in Heaven are followers of God's wisdom (4Q418).

According to the Dead Sea Scrolls, it is essential that both followers of religion and those who tend crops incorporate angels and blessings for the land. The Calendar of the Heavenly Signs shows 294-year cycles of six "jubilees" (every 49 years) marked by 'ots, or "signs," with solar-lunar conjunctions that farmers and lay people alike are to honor (4Q319). It's worth noting that these practices were occurring under the rule of a female Hebrew monarch, Shelamzion, or Alexandra, in 76 BCE, and continued until 63 BCE, when Rome conquered the Temple at Jerusalem, slaying 12,000 people.

The Gnostic Gospels: Embodying Early Christian Spiritual Female Principles

The Nag Hammadi Library is a series of scrolls containing early Christian Gnostic Gospels found in 1947, two years after the Dead Sea Scrolls. It reveals that during the three centuries after his death, some of Jesus's teachings were carried forth by the Gnostics, some of whom were disciples or relatives of Jesus. The Gnostic beliefs conflicted with the authorities in Rome, who allied with Paul's group of early Christians and threw the might of the empire against all others. As a result, the term "Gnostic," rather than being known as being "learned" (Greek *gnostikos*, from *gnōsis*, or knowledge) became instead associated with heresy. The Gnostic gospels are probably the clearest record of early Christianity, beyond the Rome-centered documents held by the Catholic church.

The Gnostics believed in reincarnation, astrology, and that souls rest in the houses of the constellations, which is not too different from what The Dead Sea Scrolls reveal about the Essenes at Qumran beliefs.

Like the Essenes, the Gnostics believed that there is a Divine spark in every human and each person can let that "light" be a guide to salvation. This is similar to the Cherokee belief of *nvwati*, that the light of Spirit lives in everything; or the Sanscrit greeting *namaste*, that the light in one honors the light, or divinity, within another.

This is amplified in the Gospel of Thomas, one of the Gnostic texts in the Nag Hammadi Library. The Gospel of Thomas includes some 114 quotes from Jesus, including: "I am the light that shines over all things. I am everything. From me all came forth, and to me all return. Split a piece of wood, and I am there. Lift a stone, and you will find me there." The Essenes, likewise, called themselves Sons of Light, and referred to Psalms 82: "I have said, Ye are gods (*elohim*); and all of you children of the most High (*oliun*)." Again, common threads of belief show the power of Spirit in all things, animate and inanimate, which is shared with indigenous beliefs worldwide, and the light of Creator foremost.

Given this view of divinity within all beings, perhaps unsurprisingly, the Gnostics believed that women were equal to men in their communities, without discrimination, including religious leadership. This "woman as co-equal" approach in all things, from society to the Divine, was a radical departure from the culture of the time. A text from the Nag Hammadi, "On the Origin of the World," expresses the Gnostic philosophy with regard to the Creator, naming the Divine Force as Sophia, which is referred to as "Her." [4] As the First Force or primal force, Sophia became "pregnant" of "Her" own accord and gave birth to matter—the first substance, water—"as with a woman giving birth to a child." The being that came forth was Yaldabaoth (Jehovah or Yahweh). Thus, all things, Jehovah, the angels, humans, Earth—everything—issued from the Womb of the Goddess Sophia.

Earthly Mother and Heavenly Father

Though it is not included in The Dead Sea Scrolls, an account called The Gospel of The Essenes refers to Jesus as describing the Earth as the "Mother" of humankind. [5] In this account, when referring to God, Jesus doesn't just use the word "Father" for the Supreme Being, he says: "Of the Earthly Mother/And the Heavenly Father," thus making the primacy of a Male/Female godhead clear. Jesus also speaks of the angels as living in water, on land, as spirits of Earth. He names which angels belong to the Father and which to the Mother, and that they should be acknowledged as "Mother's" in the morning and "Father's" in the evening.

This view of the Earthly Mother as worthy of devotion equal to the Heavenly Father is, as I noted earlier, not uncommon among ancient agrarian societies. Most early societies did view Earth as female and essential to life—all life. Without the male power, the seed, there would be no life, but without the womb there could be no life. Hence, they were different but equal, with there being no primacy of one over the other. In most early societies, as with the Essenes, the belief in the Earthly Mother and Heavenly Father as co-creators was not unusual.

This helps to explain why the patriarchal "official" church viewed rivals to Paul's teachings as needing to be eradicated. It did so quite effectively with The Council of Nicaea, convened by Roman Emperor Constantine in AD 325. Constantine was quoted as saying that the Gnostic teachings were a heretical way of thinking and were "of no practical importance." The idea that angels are coexistent in the ceremonies of the Church was banished, the time-honored agricultural feasts and festivals were stripped from holy writ, and all references to women as in any way co-equal to men were removed. Through its sweeping actions, the Council changed forever how a good portion of Western civilization now thinks about life, ourselves, our communities, our institutions, and our planet.

From that point onward, the development of Western civilization went forward without being governed by the unconditional love that is the hallmark of a female divinity and a society. Constantine's actions made the goddess nonexistent for all humankind who subscribed to Christian belief, and individually, on some level, we may feel that emptiness within us, and reflected all around us, as a spiritual hunger that cannot be quenched.

Constantine's decision, reverberating through the centuries, silenced the female voice in our modern Bible. It also effectively removed one of its Founder's most precious gifts—compassion—which, in early texts, was translated as "womb-like love," all-encompassing and nurturing, as opposed to the Old Testament's "mercy," a quality that can easily be withheld, parceled out, or denied. [6]

A Felt Imbalance

Today, the pendulum of change seems to have made its farthest swing toward the masculine, with war, division, and domination now constituting the major global themes. In order for any society to be healthy (and today it's a global one), there must be balance between polarities.

As the feminine aspect was stripped from the Divine in Judaism, Christianity, and Islam, and indigenous beliefs and peoples were subjugated, the scientific method removed divinity from subjective experience entirely. Hence, the concept of sacredness has been diminished and replaced by materialism. Both the Divine feminine and Spirit have been removed from the daily life of many. Yet, the entire known history of humankind is intimately entwined with both.

The reason Spirit is no longer associated with food is not because it doesn't belong there intrinsically, but because our society has so accentuated the male values of heroics, dominance, and war that Spirit is seen, perhaps rightly, as feminine in nature, but wrongly, to be rejected as weak or subservient.

Another factor is the separation of church and state, and how popular culture often views religion and spirituality interchangeably. As the late historian Jo Ann McNamara observed: "The Roman tradition upheld the virtues associated with male virility; the developing Christian religion (pre-Constantine) consciously urged the feminine virtues of compassion and humility on both men and women."

Millions of dollars are spent on advertising by giant multinational agribusinesses to promote a masculine, take-control image in the name of progress and the language of conquest. The "brave new world" of technology advances through chemistry and "fighting world hunger" through largely untested genetic modifications has only widened the battlefront, creating batallions of new problems to fight. It's good for business in the short term, bad for Earth in the long run.

Clearly, if we are creating new problems, we are not moving forward. The futile and ironic conquest of Nature may have as its root the fearful knowledge that Nature cannot be conquered, but we can sometimes stay a step ahead, which is a comfort of sorts. Acceptance and nurturing—archetypal feminine attributes—are needed to rein in runaway agribusiness at "war" with Earth. This does not imply passivity; it implies Right Action. As with Buddhism and other wisdom traditions, the essence of Christianity is nonviolence. So, the history of agriculture, like the history of religion, has been at odds with itself since Roman times. Denuding landscapes mechanically and chemically in order to turn around and make land bountiful with healthful, nutritious crops is as dissonant as conquering or killing "unbelievers" in order to "save" them.

Changes Afoot

Why do modern people yearn for a return to the land and feel as if they are missing something spiritually from their connection with food? Perhaps because they have lost touch with their natural selves, their ancestral stories, and their roots in ancient myth and ritual.

The yearning that so many of us feel for a "return to the earth" can be seen as acknowledgment that something is lacking in our daily lives, and the fact that crucial elements of life are missing from mainstream culture.

There are no Utopias to be found in the past, nor likely any in the future; however, the spiritual values around which some ancient societies were structured seem much more sane than our own. True, ancient traditions and rituals may have been engendered by fear of angry goddesses wreaking havoc through natural disasters, a way to appease fickle Nature, but they seem also to have sprung from a deep connection to Earth and all beings.

For tens of thousands of years, all across the globe, humankind lived in balanced societies that were tied to the seasons, with respect for elders, male and female equally, and belief systems that recognized and honored Spirit in all aspects of life, but especially in food.

When the temples were the centers of life, they were surrounded by villages and small farms. But when the warrior culture from the Caucasian Mountains and the Russian steppes spread across the Middle East, Europe, and India, the conquerors—Aryans, Indo-Europeans, and Kurgans—transformed these small agrarian societies.

Rival kings created palaces instead of temples. Male relatives formed aristocracies based on fear and war. And landowners now found themselves to be tenants and slaves.

The Celts

Called *Keltoi* and *Galatatae* by the Greeks, and *Celtae* or *Galli* by the Romans, the peoples considered Celtic (who shared a common language) extended to northern Italy from central Europe and into the British Isles. Prior to Caesar's conquest of Gaul (France) in the AD 50s, there was extensive trade with Rome. It's believed that Rome's thirst for gold prompted the invasion.

Until the Romans invaded the British Isles starting in 55 BCE, the Celtic people lived in small villages, with agriculture the central way of life, filled with festivals and respect for goddesses and fertility of the soil. The Great Mother was known by many names around the Mediterranean, including Rehe, Cybele, Demeter, Astarte, Aphrodite, Isis, and Ma. The Celtic goddess Brigit was associated with grain, the very soul of agriculture and food. The making of bread itself, from grain to flour to dough to bread, was considered an alchemy and blessing, emblematic of transformation.

Roman occupation and influence lasted just under 400 years, until about AD 410. Tacitus writes that the Celts made no distinction in the gender of their leaders and were used to women commanders in war. The most famous were Cartimandua, queen of the Brigantes, and Boudica, queen of the Iceni. Women may also have had greater rights pertaining to marriage, divorce, property ownership, and the right to rule, similar to Native American societies.

When we talk of Western culture and history, we are usually generally referring to Classical Greek and Roman times. It's not because the British Isles and European countries didn't have their own histories—they did; but the ancient Celtic peoples had their religion destroyed, their places of worship dismantled, their religious and cultural leaders killed, and their children taught the ways of Rome.

The minimizing of the value of agriculture and its historically intrinsic connection with Spirit goes hand in hand with the subjugation of women. It's no coincidence that agriculture, food, Spirit, and the role of women and elders are all marginalized in Western society. Indeed, they are of one piece: the divinity of land, food, and women has been "conquered" and relegated to lesser status. Moreover, when Europeans came to the Americas, they sought (and largely accomplished) the same annihilation of culture in their dealings with indigenous peoples that had occurred to them in the homelands they had left behind.

Ironically, this monoculture may today be a way of salvation. In some Native American societies, among medicine people, it was sometimes necessary for one to forget everything to be taught anew. Among the Cherokee, for example, certain herbs were used to "erase" memory, so that the person could be taught medicine ways. The mental slate was effectively "wiped clean."

While this could be disastrous if literally carried out in modern society, nevertheless, it's a useful allegory for approaching this new age and the next millennium. When it comes to infusing agriculture with Spirit and forging a better way of approaching food and eating, a little amnesia might be a good thing, just as selective memory—such as recalling the Divine feminine and religious connections noted here from the past—can provide an historical grounding for the future.

Now it seems, things are beginning to change all over. Communities that work together to create new dynamics of social progress and self-sufficiency that were ignored as oddball phenomena are now gaining serious media attention. Young people are going into farming and beginning to revitalize moribund rural areas. And the urban faming movement has taken off in many major cities. The stories of agriculture are being rewritten, in inclusive ways—with regard for gender equality, sustainability, and provision for elders and generations to come.

By returning Spirit to food, we create edible prayers that are healing for ourselves and our planet.

■ From Jim's Farming Notbook: Women's Small Farms Emerging

Other than "factory farms," a common organic farm nationally is 5 acres or less and earns less than $5,000—which is also the cutoff amount for annual income required to be certified organic by the U.S. Department of Agriculture—and these are thriving.

According to the Rodale Institute, 3,714 U.S. organic farms in 2008 reported under $5,000 in annual sales per farm combined, for sales of just over $7 million. These comprise 25 percent of the total number of U.S. organic farms. (As with "conventional" agriculture, corporate industrial farming predominates in the organic sector: Of the 14,540 organic farms reporting, average annual sales were $217,675, but were more profitable than conventional farms.)

Since that accounting, ever more small "backyard" farmers have begun growing food for themselves, their families, their friends, and selling to others. Small farms are actually the norm nationwide.

According to the USDA 2007 farm census, more than half of all farms in the United States were under 50 acres, nearly a quarter of a million of the 1.3 million total farms were under 10 acres. A scant 22,000 farms were over the 5,000 acres that is considered conventional farming in the United States today. The "average" farm is a small farm, not the big subsidy-eating Goliath that politicians cater to and offer subsidies for, which accounts for less than 4 percent of farms in America.

A small farm is actually more efficient than a larger one. Consider the urban gardening operation of Will Allen of Milwaukee, Wisconsin, head of Growing Power. Using abandoned lots and building his own compost from weeds and worm bins, he produces $5 per square foot income, which in his operation translates into $200,000 per acre. Of course, he also has a small army of volunteers to help. But, as Allen puts it, anything less than $5 per square foot is unsustainable as a farm operation.

In our own case, Annette and I grow fall and winter greens on a small backyard plot with artsy spiral-shaped rows. In 2010, we were selling 80–100 pounds of produce per week, at peak harvest, on a plot that is roughly 50 feet by 40 feet, or 2,000 square feet. If you figure $3 per pound for greens (wholesale), that's up to $300 per week for up to 12 weeks. That year, our plot produced about $1.80 per square foot, but it was not intensively grown, and the square footage includes the numerous walkways.

Individual growers will have to decide what's of value to them, and how intensively they intend to grow. Small, intensive, organic farmer Eliot Coleman of Four Seasons Farm in Maine estimates the largest farm that two people can manage without hired help is 2 ½-acres.

Surprisingly, and also not much noted by the media or politicians, is the skyrocketing number of farms headed by women. Between 2002 and 2007, the number grew to 306,000 (nearly a one-third increase), and the total number of acres cultivated by women in the United States grew to more than 64 million acres, with more than 56,000 farms headed by women less than 10 acres in size. That trend, no doubt, has continued since those figures were compiled. (The next census is to be conducted in 2012. For more information on U.S. women in agriculture, see: *http://www.agcensus.usda.gov/ Publications/2007/Online_Highlights/Fact_Sheets/women.pdf)*. Most new farms headed by women are in the northeastern United States (reflecting urban farming, or backyard farming, or community agriculture) and in the western United States.

Women heading farm operations is a "back-to-the-future" trend that is happening worldwide and needing only a little push. According to the Chicago Council on Global Affairs, one of the oldest and most respected international affairs organizations in the United States, girls and women in rural economies handle 43 percent of all farming. By international organizations focusing on educating adolescent girls, the group said in its 2011 report, *Girls Grow: A Vital Force in Rural Economies*, a number of groundshaking changes could occur in the world's rural economies, including:

- Women's agricultural yields could increase up to 30 percent;
- National agricultural output could increase up to 4 percent;
- The number of undernourished people could be reduced up to 17 percent.

The girls' hands-on knowledge and experience with agriculture, local crop species, and environmental conditions, along with more educational opportunities and support, could help them become "leaders in agricultural research and extension and as entrepreneurs and workers across the agricultural value chain."

This can be done through sustainable agriculture, on small plots with community support. This is the type of farming that is not reliant on foreign inputs; rather, it promotes carbon sequestration, watershed management, and the preservation of biodiversity.

The group says that the world's 283 million rural adolescent girls can help reverse the poverty of rural people and put nations on the path to food security.

The world—both in industrialized nations such as the United States as well as in rural economies—is poised to make a postmodern leap with female leadership in food resources.

■ From Jim's Farming Notebook: You Don't Have to Live in the Country to Farm

You don't have to live in the country to grow your own food. In looking at your available space, heed the experts.

Three concepts come to mind:

- "Fertility Leaks"
- "The Hidden Garden"
- "The Edible Yard"

Fertility Leaks is a concept popularized by self-described "lunatic" farmer Joel Salatin, who practices some rather innovative farming practices on his cattle ranch in the Shenandoah Valley of Virginia.

He writes that he constantly is looking for ways to better harness energy or resources that most "normal" people ignore. For example, instead of buying a new pickup truck or tractor when he gets ahead financially, he says, he uses the money to build more ponds, even if they are only 20 feet wide.

That way, in drought, he can just tap the water wherever it's needed, instead of selling off his cattle, taking out government disaster loans, and so on. He also keeps his pastures from being eroded that way, adding topsoil year after year. He makes "sustainability" more than a catchy buzzword; he lives it. For more, see his book, *The Sheer Ecstasy of Being a Lunatic Farmer* (Polyface, 2010). He also has choice words about Big Ag and government subsidies!

Fertility Leaks are everywhere. For example, most people around where we live burn their leaves every year. We compost it. Why not? It's free soil-building material. If you look around your place, you might find lots more efficiencies, as well.

The Hidden Garden is a concept advanced by intensive organic market garden pioneer Eliot Coleman. His entire operation, Four Season Farm in Maine, which is internationally known for its quality of greens grown throughout the year, is only 6 acres. (He actually has more, but it's hilly, rocky, or otherwise unsuitable for cultivation.) In 2010, Coleman reported netting about $120,000 per year on that 6 acres. But note that he farms intensively, year round, and with hired help. He's also world renowned—people come from hundreds of miles to meet him and to buy from his onsite farm stand—so there's a committed market and no transportation costs.

Coleman says that over the years he has taught himself to look at unlikely or rejected spaces for growing. For example, he plants parsley on the corners of his plots because it grows prolifically and nothing else can be easily harvested in those spots—every inch of his available space is utilized for growing. He also put his 90-foot-long greenhouses on sled runners, so that by moving them after each season, he can rotate his soil with rejuvenating cover crops and still provide produce year round.

Coleman says that some of the practices he employs derive from what's called "The French Method," popular in the 19th century, when all of Paris was fed by 2-acre market gardens. Any space that can be but is not used, he calls "The Hidden Garden," just waiting to be discovered by someone who has the creativity or vision to see it.

Finally, there is The Edible Yard, or swapping your lawn for an edible landscape, pioneered by Rosalind Creasy. Creasy's book, *The Complete Book of Edible Landscaping: Home Landscaping with Food-Bearing Plants and Resource-Saving Techniques* (Sierra Club Books,

1982), and other such popular books as *The Edible Landscape* by Tom MacCubbin (Charles B. McFadden, 1998), boosted the idea of edible landscapes, and shifting yards to make them into foodscapes has become a national movement.

Review

History of Food and Spirit:

- The Western view of the world is paternalistic, a male model, and a rejection of the Divine feminine that governed human behavior and civilization for thousands of years.
- The world is out of balance primarily because the Western worldview has tilted thoughts and behaviors.
- Rudolf Steiner recognized this loss of Spirit in the early 20th century and tried to reverse the trend, but the forces of society immediately before World War II were too strong, the impetus for world conflict too overwhelming.
- People are yearning for a return to the earth and a connection to Spirit that brings us full circle to blending the past, present, and future to form a new agriculture, a new society, a new way of viewing food, and all our relationships that flow from it.

INTERNET KEY WORDS: *Rudolf Steiner, biodynamic farming, Divine feminine, goddess religions, Essenes, Gnostics, Iroquois, matrilineal, Reiki, Shamanism, Reiki Shamanism*

CHAPTER TWO

Postmodern Organics:
A New Science for Earth

Earth is the alien planet now.
—WILLIAM GIBSON

There are many timelines, which theorists call "overlays" of reality. At any moment, reality can change from many potentials. This is the reality the medicine person perceives and that creates "miracles"—that Creator will allow the best reality for those affected, if approached in a sacred manner. This does not go against Creator's will; instead, it brings human will in line with Divine will, so that both may be closer and act as one. It's not far-fetched. Bringing overlays into reality is what we do when we decide to take a right turn going to work in the morning instead of left. We may be delayed, or maybe we arrive early, so that our boss sees us and decides to give us a bonus. Overlays are simply choices in potential for reality to fill.

When you set your intent upon the highest and best outcome regarding a situation or a set of facts, the hologram of 3-D reality, the story, can be changed. This "magic" is simply moving one outcome over another in probability. We can help balance our world by the concepts we hold in our minds. We can revisit the memory of these ancestor ways that actually included men, women, and elders as equals, that actively valued children, the infirm, and all beings of Earth as being important and worth protecting. When we hold these values our decisions change, followed by our behaviors—first as individuals, then as groups, then as nations. We create the reality we value and hold in our hearts and minds. (For more on prayers and reality, see my books *Finding Sanctuary in Nature* and *Healing Plants & Animals From a Distance*.)

Already, worldwide, there is a *de facto* shift in roles and decision-making that might be termed "matrifocal," in which women, especially mothers, are increasingly occupying a central position, though perhaps not noticed in the popular media. This is particularly true in Western economics, where women make the majority of the day-to-day buying decisions, especially regarding food. In modern consumer culture, she who controls the purse strings decides the course of society.

It just so happens that spiritual issues and decisions regarding childcare and health care are also the major areas of influence of women in society. This synergy of food, health, and spirit is growing, even if it's off the radar of political decision-makers at present.

As I've briefly recounted in Chapter 1, the way of viewing the world in terms of Spirit is thousands of years old, allied with a balanced view of society, which itself depends on agriculture— food!— for its very existence. And science, heretofore perhaps seen as the enemy of Spirit, is poised to merge with a postmodern way of looking at the food we put into our bodies. The result will be a new agriculture for Planet Earth, a new science that brings Spirit, Art, and, yes, Love, Reverence, Gratitude, and Respect into the equation. It is a return of the Divine feminine, of balance and harmony, to the earth, rejecting the patrimony of unbridled aggression, scarcity, and want.

Around the world, people are working to reinvent traditional ways of growing food, even as government-funded international distribution systems and seed ownership by multinational corporations are limiting the means for growing heirloom seeds or promoting local and sustainable crops. The battle cry—for indeed it *is* a battle for corporate control of food and the means for producing food—is that "science must feed the world." But there is no fight between true science and sustainability. Scientific inquiry does not in any way threaten locally, sustainable food, but rather, supports it.

So, why do those who support government and corporate control of food wave the banner of science, painting people who can verifiably and scientifically prove local, organic, and ecological farming provides sustainable, safe, and abundant crops as Luddites standing in the way of progress?

Perhaps because returning control of food and food production to the people themselves is an unprofitable idea in many ways. It's much easier for a powerful few to control the many through economics if they have control of the food supply. If anyone, and everyone, can grow healthful, nutritious food in their backyards, on their windowsills, or in their neighborhood community gardens, or have access to locally grown, chemically free fruit and vegetables, where is the profit? These people might even get healthy and need fewer drugs and less expensive medical care. A purer form of democracy, where voices for sustainability count, communities are more self-sufficient, and corporations hold right-side-up values, is necessary for our survival.

Agriculture is the foundation of our civilization. The return to agrarian ideals and firm beliefs in the power of individuals, groups, and neighborhoods to restore community will gradually unravel concentration of political and economic power. Our food choices really do make a difference. Citizens, farmers, consumers, churches, and communities can make a difference by their informed choices and by actively doing.

The separation of Spirit from food was the primary reason that agriculture—and with it, respect for food—lost its status at the center of life, as part of the home and the basis of civilization; food had become a mere commodity. The Roman view of conquest and male hegemony reduced the food we put into our bodies from a Spirit-based form of respect for the earth and honoring ourselves to a commodity controlled by a few for the benefit of a few, holding the rest in thrall.

In all the ancient societies of the Earth, food was prayed over, and growing it was a spiritual practice. These were edible prayers people were growing, and they helped peaceful societies based on equality, respect, and social responsibility to flourish. Human beings have the opportunity now to rebalance, beginning with individual choices that become societal choices.

According to the Organic Consumers Association, "Consumers aren't sure today's agriculture still qualifies as farming." Why? Some answers include: generational and geographic distance between farmers and consumers, technological advances in farming, and changes in farm size and structure. Consumer alienation from agriculture and the food system is expressed through concerns about nutrition, food safety, affordability, environmental sustainability, animal welfare, and other issues.

This depersonalization is the "new normal" of today's agriculture, and the shift of ever more alienation, of farming as spiritless, mechanical industry, and not a personal, intimate relationship with food, is increasing worldwide.

Big Ag and Disappearing Small Towns

In 1900, U.S. Census Bureau records show that 41 percent of Americans were employed on farms; by 2000, that number had fallen to 1.9 percent, most of the loss occurring since World War II. In the 21st century, a relative handful of ever larger industrial farms produce the majority of food, and rural areas have become depopulated, with less than one-quarter of the nation's population now living there, down from nearly half.

An entire generation in America has lost its roots and even the wherewithal to grow its own food because food production and distribution is managed by fewer and fewer hands. Conventional farming is supported by universities, in that their programs are funded by multinationals that pay for the grants, scholarships, and research to prove their methods and products are superior. We know that these methods are environmentally untenable—and support the food industry that produces more "food products" than real, healthy food. Yet, this is the model being pushed by government-supported industry and multinational banking systems as the one to "feed the world."

These propagandas of unsustainable agriculture come as the world is also confronting the effects of climate change. Some credible evidence, such as that outlined by author Bill McKibben in his book *Eaarth*, even seems to back up the theory that our planet has become a new planet—one that no longer conforms to the old, measurable seasons, with increasing atmospheric carbon changing the very nature of, well, Nature, and therefore necessitating a new name. In a sense, we do live on an alien planet from that of our forebears, where Spirit is separated from food.

Soil: At the Root of Postmodern Agriculture

Steiner's Agriculture Course in the early 20th century was the last gasp of an attempt to reconcile food and Spirit with the growing juggernaut of mechanized farming, synthetic and toxic chemical application to the land, and an industrialized food system that valued quantity and profit over quality and nutrition.

Until Rachel Carson published her book *Silent Spring* in 1962, few doubted the wonders of chemical pesticides. Principal among these was DDT, which took years to build toxicity in the bodies of those exposed to it and to work its way up the food chain. It was scientifically proven to be effective and, with limited test subjects, safe. That is, until toxic levels began to build in wildlife populations and dieoffs began. Today, it seems, many have forgotten the lesson of

DDT and the prescient warning of *Silent Spring*—that science in the marketplace needs monitoring and continuing inquiry that closes no doors to the truth.

The reliance on chemicals for farming in the post–World War II world was viewed as "modern." I suggest a *post*modern appreciation of agriculture that recognizes some of the practices by our forebears. Pre-modern people knew certain practices worked; but didn't know why. These practices can now be understood scientifically and form a persuasive argument against mechanized, synthetic growing.

For example, in 1792, Thomas Jefferson, while serving as U.S. secretary of state in Philadelphia, received a letter from his daughter, Martha, complaining about the insect-riddled plants in the Monticello vegetable garden. His response, according to Peter Hatch, director of Gardens and Grounds at the Thomas Jefferson Foundation, is a stirring anthem to sustainable practices: "We will try this winter to cover our garden with a heavy coating of manure," Jefferson wrote. "When it is rich it bids defiance to droughts, yields in abundance, and of the best quality. I suspect that the insects which have harassed you have been encouraged by the feebleness of your plants; and that has been produced by the lean state of the soil." [1]

Reliance upon cultivating soil with natural amendments for the health of plants is now basic to organic agriculture.

Artificial Fertilizers

The history of what is known as husbandry in Europe and America prior to the Industrial Revolution, going back to ancient Egypt, Greek, Roman and Anglo-Saxon times, has been well chronicled by the late Sir Albert Howard (1873–1947). Howard railed against the loss of fertility in soil as the result of what is now called "conventional" agriculture. His thoughts, along with those of Bob Rodale, and J. I. Rodale, who died in 1971, are considered foundational to the modern organic movement.

Many people today may not be aware that the common usage of NPK (nitrogen, potassium, and phosphorous) and the three numbers on the side of chemical fertilizer bags that describe their content, such as 12-12-12, is a relatively new phenomenon.

The idea, or "discovery" as it was called, that plants could thrive on only these three elements originated with Justus von Liebig (1803–1873), known as "the father of the fertilizer industry." But it wasn't until German chemist Fritz Haber (1868–1934) invented a way to synthesize large quantities of nitrogen, using what's known as the Haber-Bosch Process, that chemical fertilizer found a foothold. Haber was awarded the Nobel Prize for Chemistry in 1918, but was also known as the "father of chemical warfare" during World War I.

The widespread conversion from natural methods to the selective applications of synthetic chemicals in "conventional" farming is allied with war, as are many technological advances throughout history. After World War II, the infrastructure was in place for making nitrogen for bombs; it was a simple change to use this existing process to shift to producing bags of fertilizer. Bombs to fertilizer, beating swords into plowshares, seemed a natural process. Not everyone supported this "new" method of growing crops, however, chief among them Sir Albert Howard, who produced his own experiments showing that natural methods could equal production in the long term.

As most modern farmers who have used chemical fertilizers have found, yields at first are boosted, but the chemicals eventually compromise biological activity in the soil and ruin its structure, making it essentially lifeless. As farmers continue to farm using artificial methods, they must use higher amounts of fertilizer, which adds costs per acre. But as more fertilizer is used, it seems to weaken plant immunological response, which also necessitates using more chemicals to fight plant diseases and insects. The result, ultimately, is that crops are grown in a chemical soup that depletes the soil, lowers nutritional value, and can result in desertification (such as the Dust Bowl of the 1930s) and buildup of salts in the soil that makes it unproductive.

Thousands of acres in California are now unsuitable for farming because of this process, and some point to the ancient Native American civilization of the Hohokam as an example of where modern farming is headed. For 1,000 years, the sophisticated Hohokam culture maintained more than 300 miles of irrigation canals to water their fields in what is now the state of Arizona. Some estimates have placed the peak Hohokam population in the Phoenix, Arizona, area at more than 250,000 people. But sometime before AD 1450, the civilization collapsed—the name Hohokam itself is a Pima Indian word meaning "those who are gone."

Among the modern explanations for the collapse of Hohokam civilization are that their monoculture way of growing failed, creating desertification and starving the local population, causing their descendants to abandon agriculture and go back to hunting and gathering. It's a grim reminder, especially as this "modern" monoculture way of faming has been adopted worldwide. The United Nations Convention to Combat Desertification estimates that since 1950 some 4.7 billion acres of land has been made unfit for farming globally.

Healthy Soil

Healthy, productive soil is rich with organic matter called humus, formed when decaying plants and animals are transformed by microorganisms and fungi; it's rich in carbon, NPK, and other essential nutrients, as well as trace elements such as sulphur, boron, and calcium. And it has what's called "tilth," or loft, good, crumbly soil structure, often accentuated by the presence of earthworms, which allow air to circulate at the root level. This substance is not the sterile, lifeless substrate found where monocultures of crops are farmed by conventional methods, where chemicals are sprayed to grow one select crop, such as corn, and all else is killed.

Do you know that smell of freshly turned earth? That's actually the odor of actinomycetes, or fungi-like bacteria. Soil repeatedly dosed with chemicals lacks that odor and the moist, crumbly texture of living soils. Obviously, crops *will* grow in sterile environments with the addition of chemicals and appear lush, as Justus von Liebig discovered in the 19th century and post–World War II industrialists exploited in the 20th century. However, we have learned the long-term effects of these practices: destruction of the soil leading to erosion, poisoning of beneficial organisms, pollution of the water table, and damage to ecosystems caused by runoff of nitrogen fertilizers.

Growth of Organics

In the United States, the Department of Agriculture officially began oversight of crops grown organically with the signing into law of the Organic Foods Production Act of 1990, authorizing a National Organic Program. By that time, thousands of farms were already employing organic methods—the California Certified Organic Farmers group, for example, had been founded in 1973. The European Union, Canada, and Japan also have comprehensive organic legislation.

Since the Organic Foods Production Act, organic sales in the United States have shown unparalleled growth, from $1 billion in 1990 to $26.7 billion, a decade later. Even so, it amounted to only 4 percent of overall sales, according to the Organic Trade Association, an industry trade group.

The Rodale Institute began its own continuing Farming Systems Trial in 1981, demonstrating that organic farming produces the same yields of corn and soybeans as does conventional farming but uses 30 percent less energy, less water, and no chemicals. In addition, a comparison between organic and conventional cropping systems shows that organic/regenerative agriculture systems reduce carbon dioxide, a major greenhouse gas, and significantly decrease reliance on petrochemicals.

This could have profound implications for climate change. If all 3.5 billion acres of farmland on the planet were farmed organically, the soil would sequester nearly 40 percent of the world's carbon dioxide (CO^2) emissions, Rodale reports. And converting all 434 million acres of U.S. farmland to organic would sequester nearly 1.6 billion tons of CO^2 per year, the equivalent of taking 800,000 cars off the road annually.

Feeding the World

Despite claims by industry-backed studies and organizations that promote conventional farm systems, organic systems *can* "feed the world."

A special report released by the United Nations in March 2011, titled *Agro-ecology and The Right to Food,* reported that organic growing can sustainably double food production in entire regions within 10 years, while mitigating climate change and alleviating rural poverty. As a result, it concluded that nation states should make a fundamental shift towards agro-ecology as a more sustainable system to both feed themselves while also addressing climate change and poverty.

Yet, multinational agribusinesses seem to be successfully selling the idea that only chemical methods can support growing populations; even as the world's seven billion humans are already undernourished on a massive scale under the 70-year-old failed experiment of "conventional" farming.

Author Barry Estabrook did an exhaustive review of all the scientific literature published between 1999 and 2007 addressing the question of whether or not organic agriculture could feed the world. He notes that the British Soil Association, which supports and certifies organic farms in the United Kingdom, found that there had been 98 papers published in the previous eight years addressing the question of whether organic could feed the world. Every one of the papers showed that organic farming had that potential. Not one argued otherwise. [2]

Around the globe, more people are growing food wherever they live, with Spirit, interdependence, and communal ideals, as exemplified by the urban agriculture movement. The United Nations Development Program recently reported that an astonishing 800 million people worldwide are now engaged in urban agriculture, producing 15–20 percent of the world's food. That percentage will increase as a new generation of young people recognizes that attempts by multinational corporations to monopolize seed ownership and manipulate markets to benefit industrial farms is untenable, short-sighted, and undemocratic. Local food movements will continue to flourish in this environment. Perhaps it's time to recognize there is life, after all, in the farm fields; and in more ways than previously thought.

Consciousness in Plants

While scientific discoveries have brought awareness of the building blocks of synthetic agriculture, they have also demonstrated hidden links that show we still have much to learn about the biology of plants.

It has long been known that plants have a kind of basic consciousness, heliotropism, first described by Leonardo da Vinci (1452–1519). Heliotropism is the movement of certain plants to face and follow the sun throughout the day.

The book *The Secret Life of Plants* (HarperPerennial, 1973), written by Peter Tompkins and Christopher Bird and turned into a popular documentary in 1979, showed that plants also respond to human emotions. The book drew on the experience of an FBI polygraph expert and trainer, Cleve Backster, who, in 1966, using adapted polygraphs (machinery used for lie-detector tests), found that not only do plants react to physical events around them but also when they were merely threatened with injurious thoughts; they even responded to angry emotions or disturbances beyond their physical presence. The plants reacted positively to events such as receiving water, even before the water was given. He documented that plants react with what can only be described as conscious awareness, and can even respond to the thoughts of people within and outside their energy field.

Belief that plants respond to thoughts goes back even farther, to the Indian scientist Sir Jagdish Chandra Bose, who conducted similar experiments on plants in 1900, and even before that to Dr. Gustav Theodor Fechner, a German professor, in 1848. But it wasn't until sophisticated technology emerged to measure this scientifically that a body of knowledge began to accrue.

In the 1940s, Dr. Harold S. Burr at Yale University measured electrical conductivity and mapped the energy fields around living plants and animals. He found that a salamander has an energy field around it. What was particularly surprisingly, though, was that this held true also for an unfertilized salamander egg, which Burr found also had an energy field around it that corresponded roughly to the shape of the adult salamander.

Also in the 1940s, a Russian researcher, Semyon Kirlian, discovered that when a portion of a leaf is cut off, the remaining leaf has an energy field that continues to show the whole uncut leaf. He called this The Phantom Leaf Effect. Refining the measurement techniques, Ion Dumitrescu in Romania found that the energy field was so precise as to even include the intricate patterns of the veins on the back side of the missing leaf part. Burr also found that plants react to the movements of the sun, moon, tides, and planets, showing they are intimately connected to and aware of their environment.

While all of these studies have suggested there is "something there," formulating clear tests to measure that "something" has been difficult, because plants can't respond in spoken words to the exact source of stimuli to which they may be reacting, or which they may be ignoring. A picture is emerging, however, that considerably more communication is occurring in farm fields (or in garden pots on the patio or windowsill) than previously thought, and which, in various ways, is difficult to detect, even with sophisticated devices.

Weeds and Bugs: Friends or Foes?

Plants and insects have coexisted quite well throughout time, a fact that modern chemical control systems seem to ignore, but postmodern approaches embrace. Each has defense mechanisms against the other, and both are constantly changing to seek an advantage. As a result, even crop scientists trying to selectively poison both plants and insects are constantly behind the curve in creating ever more effective toxins.

Some eco-farmers work with Nature and use the plants' own toxins to grow crops. For example, within 24–48 hours after germination, weed seeds emit auxins (plant hormones or plant growth substances) that chemically tell other nearby species to stay asleep in the soil. With thousands of weed seeds per square foot, it's Nature's way of controlling plant populations. Once these roots are visible, those who practice organic methods know they can till the soil again (changing the oxygen makeup) and plant their own seeds and have weeds subdued by their own biological methods.

Weeds, far from being enemies of farmers, can be a great ally, as the late Charles Walters, founder of *Acres USA* magazine, pointed out in his book *Weeds: Control Without Poisons* (Acres USA, 1999).

While some weeds thrive only where there is an excess of certain minerals and reduce it by growing there, other weeds proliferate where certain soil nutrients are lacking and by themselves produce that nutrient. Nature always seeks balance.

Many farmers who practice organic growing methods are well aware of this natural principle and its many manifestations. For example, a plant species may invade a field, only to be decimated by an insect that is attracted to that plant. Similarly, an insect may appear to totally be out of control and later be decimated by another predator insect to bring balance to the field. For this reason, rather than relying on pesticides to control insects and killing all of them, natural and organic growers may introduce beneficial insects, such as ladybugs, praying mantids, and certain wasps, and intersperse beneficial bug habitats throughout their growing areas that can balance infestations in crops.

A subject that eluded growers for centuries was determining how insects learned to zero in on certain plants. In 1859, an Irishman named John Tyndall came up with a theory, and in the process, predicted climate change by more than a century and a half.

Tyndall posited that even small quantities of water vapor, carbon dioxide, and ozone are the best absorbers of heat radiation, and that the fluctuations of these three change the Earth's temperature. He also speculated in his 1863 book, *Heat Considered as a Mode of Motion* (Adamant, 2001), that scent molecules from flowers and plants absorb infrared light, including from the sun, moon and stars, providing a map for insects to determine the health of those plants.

Communications Systems in the Garden

Tyndall was ignored by modern scientists until recent years, when his discoveries all of a sudden made sense. Phillip S. Callahan, a former U.S. Department of Agriculture Insect Biophysics specialist and

University of Florida professor, expanded on Tyndall's studies, proving that plants and insects communicate through emissions in the infrared frequency range. In his book, *Tuning In to Nature: Infrared Radiation and the Insect Communication System* (Devin-Adair, 1976), he showed how plants under stress literally signal insects to come devour them.

Just as insects release pheromones for mating, Callahan showed that plants release scents based on their health. The scents then absorb radiation, releasing a signature frequency, and the insects, through their antennae, detect these frequencies and follow them. At short range, they use sensilla, or short spines on their bodies, to read the signals.

Modern agricultural scientists have used this information to track the types of insects living among crops so as to determine which pesticides to spray. But there's a greater dimension to this, which is easily overlooked.

As Callahan also proved, every living thing on the planet, including weeds, trees, insects, and humans, has what's called "blackbody" radiation—coherent energy waves based on its peak temperature that are unique to it. Indeed, if we had instruments sensitive enough, we could look into a landscape, and even across it into a city, and observe the mental and physical conditions of all beings—we could know their health, their interests, their psychology, whether they are nervous or at rest, feeling excited or introverted, or asleep, as well as the conditions of their pets, their plants, and their environs. And it would be extremely detailed information, based on scent and transmitted via radiowaves, for all who can detect it to see for themselves.

As noted, plants also communicate in ways that aren't well understood, as polygraph expert and trainer Cleve Backster and others proved, and via seed auxins sending chemical messages. Neurobiologists have also discovered that plants also have rudimentary neurological networks and the capacity for primary perceptions. Some, for example, eat insects by closing their leaves when they land on them, or close when they detect other insects, such as ants coming to steal their nectar; others send out blasts of scent when they are being eaten that warn surrounding plants.

This plant-to-plant communication is occurring all the time. In fact, researchers at Colorado State University working with the U.S. Department of Homeland Security have developed plants that subtly change color when exposed to minute amounts of explosives in the air. They are redesigned to drain off chlorophyll—the compound that makes them green—from leaves, blanching to white when bomb materials are detected.

But that's just the tip of the iceberg. The earth itself is communicating, down to the cellular level, discernible through what scientists are calling "quorum sensing." It is a process by which bacteria communicate with each other about how they should behave collectively. Specifically, bacteria in the soil release signaling molecules, which bind to specific receptors on other bacteria and pass the required message. The density of signaling molecules helps the bacteria sense the size of the population (quorum), thus the name. Collectively, this allows colonies of bacteria to manipulate their genetic structure to meet changing conditions. In some circles, the ability to perceive and act upon information gathered and transmitted is characterized by a more common description: sentient life.

This ability of bacteria to communicate raises questions about our soil structures (which are commonly destroyed by chemical farming). For example, mycorrhizal fungi form extensive networks below the surface of the soil that connect the roots of many plant species into an integrated system. While researchers have determined that this subterranean labyrinth provides pathways for nutrient exchange among different plant species, they aren't exactly sure how or to what extent, or even (as in the case of the quorum sensing abilities of bacteria) the type or quantity of information that is exchanged.

Scientists have only in recent years come to appreciate mycorrhizal fungi as one of the oldest forms of life on Earth. From the Greek words *mykos* for "fungus" and *rhizon* for "root," mycorrhizal fungi earned their name because 19th-century scientists noted that fungus was commonly found in roots, but at the time, they didn't understand that it was the fungal root network that is essential to optimum growth.

The fungus actually extends the root action and efficiency of the plant, helping it obtain phosphorous from the soil, while the fungus is dependent on the plant for its optimal health. This mutual symbiosis predates human beings, going back to the breakup of the supercontinent of Pangaea, 225 million years ago, during which time plants lived in large associations that extended many miles.

The movie *Avatar* featured a "living" planet, Pandora, in which all life was interconnected. Perhaps that is not so far-fetched, but may instead be a hidden model of the world in which we live. Researchers have also found unrelated microbes that communicate through nanoscopic electronic networks—an interspecies swapping of electrons.

Moreover, simple organisms in the soil, as well as those that have symbiotic relationships, may be evolving much faster than human and other animal species. Humans evolve by vertical gene transfer, which means they hand down genes from the parents to children. But the denizens of soil, rock, and ocean evolve through lateral gene transfer, that is, they share genes with one another. The organisms that use this method of growth and development actually carry within them loads of foreign and ancient genes.

This lateral gene transfer is also how scientists discovered how to create mutagenic, or genetically modified, crops, albeit clumsily, through hit and miss, and perhaps dangerously inserting genes from animals, for example, into plants. Many people are convinced that this genetic modification of organisms (GMO) may have repercussions for plant and animal species that could prove catastrophic for life on this planet. Yet, regulation is lacking, and the government of the United States has become a partner with the private corporations that pursue this type of crop science, attempting to force other countries to accept such GMO plant products, whether they want them or not. Certified organic farm production bans the use of these types of seeds and plants, but cross-contamination of organic crops is a growing problem.

There are trillions more organisms within the earth than upon its two-thirds water or one-third rocky or soil surface or the thin sheet of air surrounding it. The networks these organisms use to communicate are just as sophisticated as the neurons within the human species, but much less understood. This web of awareness is what philosophers through the ages have long sensed, and has given rise to the sentience of Earth as a being, with the Gaia theory. The question is not *if* there is knowledge, sentience, or awareness, but *how* it is perceived, or measured. People with highly developed connections to their natural self are able to "see" and "feel" Earth's energies through extrasensory means.

What does all this mean?

The discovery of the scientific basis of the perceptions of plants and insects adds credence to the theory of morphogenic fields, from the Greek *morphe,* which means "form," and *genesis,* which means "coming into being." As English author and scientist Rupert Sheldrake has explained in his book, *Morphic Resonance: The Nature of Formative Causation* (Park Creek Press, 2009), and other books, morphogenic fields encode the basic pattern of an object—in this case, detected in the infrared spectrum as measurable, unique blackbodies. Extending this a bit, morphogenic theory explains how noncorporeal beings manifest into the 3-D world: through morphogenic resonance.

We may not be able to readily see the infrared signatures of plants or animals, but they are there—just as we may not be able to detect the presence of noncorporeal beings, except in altered states of consciousness, such as the shamanic journey, a meditative or trance state. This is another step toward measuring the immeasurable: Spirit. It becomes a practical understanding when adding energetic modalities to evolving eco-farming techniques.

Blending Old and New Science

Eco-farming is a growing force in local food production worldwide, often infused with Spirit-based systems including, but not limited to, biodynamic farming based on the principles of Rudolf Steiner.

An example from Japan is that of the One Straw Revolution of natural farming, underway since 1975, when Masanobu Fukuoka (1913–2008) first published his book, *The One-Straw Revolution: An Introduction to Natural Farming* (NYRB Classics, 2010). Fukuoka believed that natural farming is tied to the spiritual health of the individual, and his growing methods were influenced by Zen Buddhism, Taoism, and the Bible. He developed his method of "do-nothing"farming, that is, allowing Nature to shape his growing methods, over 30 years. His way of farming is based on two main observations:

- Japan grew food on the same land with excellent results for 1,500 years, without artificial fertilizer or deep plowing or chemical herbicides, insecticides, or other poisons. These fields "have now been laid waste by the exploitive farming practices of a single generation."

- Left to its own devices, soil will always be replenished by Nature: weeds, animals, brush, and trees. There is no need for fertilizer or chemicals to kill insects or weeds.

The success of Fukuoka's method is based on his looking at agricultural practices from the ground up, so to speak. For example, he grew rice on dry land, rather than flooded fields, because he showed that he could produce as great a yield without all the effort involved in flooding the fields. The reason fields had been flooded since the practice began 1,500 years ago was to reduce weeds. Fukuoka found that he could achieve the same results by planting white clover, with the beneficial result of adding fertility to the soil. His four principles were:

- **No Cultivation:** It merely stirs up deeply buried weed seeds, promotes erosion and loss of topsoil, and disturbs the activity of microorganisms, small animals, and earthworms.
- **No Chemical Fertilizers Or Prepared Compost:** Left to itself, the soil maintains its fertility naturally, Fukuoka says. He did, however, return his plant chaff or straw to the ground and apply some manure.
- **No Weeding By Tillage Or Herbicides:** Weeds balance the biological community.
- **No Dependence On Chemicals:** "Nature, left alone, is in perfect balance," Fukuoka said. If even one poison is used, it can upset the balance and have catastrophic consequences. Sturdy crops grow in a healthy environment.

Those who practice organic methods will recognize these principles as, essentially, what has been called "deep organic," or growing without chemical inputs of any kind, even those approved by governments for certified organic food production.

Some of Fukuoka's methods were, of course, constrained by the types of crops he grew and the climate in which he lived. But his approach, and the methods he used, should be enlightening to anyone who seeks to grow food crops naturally.

His criticism of the inadequacy of science—particularly the slow progress of agri-scientists to explore any natural processes or systems, rather than chemical, biological, and genetic solutions—was on target. Modern research, he said, is compartmentalized and does not view the growing of crops holistically. "The results are arranged for the convenience of research, not for the needs of the farmer," he said.

Permaculture

This philosophy of farming employing naturalistic systems is also exemplified by the growing permaculture movement. The term "permaculture" was coined by Australian Bill Mollison, while a lecturer at the University of Tasmania, and David Holmgren, one of his students, to incorporate two concepts: "Permanent Culture" and "Permanent Agriculture." Mollison said the concept came to him in 1959 while watching two marsupials browsing in the rain forests. He saw how the relationship between flora and fauna was naturally sustainable. Since then, the term has grown to include a lot more than agriculture or gardening, embracing even political activity and international problem-solving.

In agriculture, the clearest way of understanding the concept would be to consider alternate phrases that essentially mean the same thing, such as eco-gardening, or creating an ecological or biodiverse garden with few human interventions. Many of the practices of organic farming, such as nurturing natural insect, fungus, and bacterial life in the soil, which promotes vegetative decomposition and encourages beneficial insects to keep balance in the garden, are elements of permaculture. But, while organic gardeners may attempt to till the soil as little as possible, disturbed ground is anathema in permaculture, since it allows nonnative invasives (or opportunistic plants) to spring forth, altering the ecosystem.

As a farming technique, it is still in its infancy but is fast growing. Now, growers around the world are developing systems of permaculture to produce food in a sustainable natural way. It's possible, as the official "organic" title has become a legal term and increasingly adopted—and manipulated—by multinational corporations, that small "deep organic" farmers will edge into more permaculture solutions to retain the original goals and spirit of "organic" as a healthy, nonchemical, sustainable way of producing food.

Along those lines, as Wes Jackson, founder of The Land Institute in Salina, Kansas, has pointed out, it was a mere accident that agriculture began with annual plants 10,000 years ago. As the Ice Age ended, pockets of fertility such as the Tigris and Euphrates Valley emerged. The first foodstuffs readily available were cereal grains, which sprouted as annuals (meaning they must be planted every year). Those seeds were readily available, abundant, and easy to transport to far-off regions.

But just as easily, our ancestors could have chosen perennials (plants that return year after year). Had they done so, the nature of agriculture would be far different, and easier on the environment. That's what The Land Institute is in the process of developing: natural seeds for perennial foodstuffs. Imagine fields of grain that are not cut down, but picked—fruits that bear year after year from the same stalks. There would be no more tilling the soil or spraying poisons; instead, there we would plant "companion" plants that provide shade or nutrients to the soil that complement the needs of the crop.

Grass Farming

This rejection of "conventional" farming has also invaded the heartland of the United States, with such well-known proponents of "grass farming" as Joel Salatin. He calls himself a "lunatic farmer" because he bases his farming activities on common sense. He allows pigs to "express their pigness," by coordinating feeding and manure production humanely, allows chickens to range in fields within moveable protective enclosures, and sets cows loose on carefully rotated fields to allow "mob feeding," which approximates how ruminants range in wild settings. Since "conventional" agriculture is considered the norm, he concludes he must be "insane" to practice farming as he believes God intended.

Eco-farmers who practice grass farming are primarily cattle producers who cultivate the soil, for what goes into the plant goes into the cow, and in turn, goes into the human body through the grass-fed meat. Meat produced in a pasture, rather than force-fed grain in confinement, was the norm in America before industrialized farming (and still practiced in most of the world). According to the Mayo Clinic, grass-fed beef is lower in calories and has lower total fat, has less fat (marbling) in the muscle of the animal, and contains more heart-healthy Omega 3 fatty acids (the "good" fat) and less Omega 6 fatty acids, which are too abundant in our diets today. It has more cancer-fighting antioxidant vitamins, such as vitamin E, and more conjugated linoleic acid (CLA), a type of fat that's thought to reduce heart disease and cancer risks.

In every sense of the word, grass farming is organic—systemic or holistic—providing nutritious food literally from the ground up and the inside out. It's also a main theme in such popular farm publications as *Acres USA* and *The Stockman Grass Farmer*.

Organic and eco-farmers, generally, might more accurately be called "dirt farmers," in the strictest sense of the term: it's all about the soil. Good soil produces good plants; poor soil, pumped up by synthetic means, does not remain that way for long. It's particularly galling to see purportedly "scientific" studies that take one plant and dump synthetic fertilizer on it, spray it with pesticides and herbicides, then take another plant and leave it alone and call it "organic." Naturally, the "conventional" agriculture plant thrives compared to the one that is left alone. But that's a false measure. There's nothing "organic" about a neglected plant in poor soil. Nurturing the soil to produce optimal growing conditions is basic to organic or eco-farming.

Finding a Spiritual Way

The spiritual aspect of farming really enters the picture when it comes time to consider the types of "amendments" to be used, as with biodynamic farming, or with activities associated with growing, such as employing activities to raise the vibration rate of the growing environment. A third, but possibly allied form of enhancing the spiritual aspect, which is actually part of the Steiner's original method but perhaps often overlooked, is employing or following spiritual guidance directly from Divine beings — as has been world made famous by the Findhorn community in Scotland.

We are—all of us—of one being. As difficult as it may seem to understand with the modern mindset of dividing knowledge into smaller and smaller, discrete bits of information, holistically we all are one. This is the ancient knowledge at the mystic heart of all cultures, whether we are speaking of Eastern mysticism or traditional Native American wisdom. We each have our own ego or personality, but that's only one part of what makes each of us who we are. We share our world, in all its various dimensions.

Ancient peoples understood this, and it's exemplified in one way with the practice of employing "biochar," a type of charcoal, for crops.

As noted in my book, *Healing Plants & Animals from a Distance* (Findhorn Press, 2007), when the first Europeans came to the Americas, they were amazed at the parklike qualities of the forests. Native Americans routinely practiced controlled burning to keep brush down and to reduce wildfires from deadwood that would destroy villages and food sources. They kept meadows and fields open by burning, as well, but they didn't "slash and burn," as did Europeans; rather, they used a process called "slash and char." That is, early Americans didn't completely burn the vegetable matter, but scorched it to make charcoal and then stirred it into the soil, creating what's called *terra preta* throughout the Americas. In this process, they used low-intensity fires—reportedly so cool they could be walked through—that would improve the soil and make more efficient use of the carbon in plants.

As a result of this carefully cultivated low-biomass fire-making, the soil was left with more "plant-available" phosphorus, calcium, sulphur, and nitrogen than commonly found—often with rich, black, fertile soil, layer upon layer, six feet deep. They also worked in turtle, fish, and animal bones as a "compost" from their food. Organic matter "sticks" to charcoal, rather than being washed away or attaching to other compounds, so over time, it partly oxidizes for nutrients to bind to, providing persistent fertility. In addition, the process doesn't release much carbon into the atmosphere, a cause of climate change—a lesson the modern world should heed.

In the scientific way of viewing the world, employing biochar with crops is typically seen as an "input," or simply an agricultural practice. But as we have seen with the belief systems of agricultural peoples throughout time, from prehistoric peoples to the Essenes to the Gnostics to Native America, agricultural practices are not seen as separate mechanical activities but as outgrowths of a spiritual belief system and an interaction with the soil as a living being--an essential part of the community itself.

In this view of the world, a corn kernel is not a seed but a "relative," entrusted to the People. It exists not only in this time but in all time, as a gift from immortal beings from the time before time to the present, so that humans might survive and thrive through eternity. The elders of the communities were taught to respect the life within them and around them, and to make sure all decisions regarding the community were considered for their impact upon the next generations. Thus, continuity of the social system was maintained, in harmony with the seeds and plants that provided food for the people.

The artifacts that are found composted into the soil where ancient peoples live—turtle, fish, and animal bones—were not rationalized soil amendments but gifts back to the Earth Mother; the animals came from Earth and were reverently returned to Earth, so that the Sacred Hoop of Life could be made complete. Enriching the soil was the result of reverence and respect and the spiritual obligation of humankind. The modern world seems mostly oblivious to its role in the Sacred Hoop of Life; its duty to give back what has been taken, so that the circle can remain unbroken and cycle an abundance of life for all beings. Taking without giving is a trait that impoverishes soil as well as individual human worth, dignity, integrity, and social systems.

The production of biochar by indigenous peoples was a spiritual activity that defined the synergistic relationships among individual humans, their societies, the plant and animal nations that fed them, and their responsibility to Earth in replenishing growing systems so all could live and thrive.

Science today is almost able to see that life in microcosm can be life in macrocosm when living in harmony with Earth, and that our role as stewards of Earth is part of a universal hologram that extends well beyond our imagining.

Biochar Holographic of Earth Consciousness

David Yarrow, a biochar reseacher who has long urged the practice in modern agriculture, offers scientific examples of the importance of biochar in his writings. In the May 2011 edition of *Acres USA* magazine, he noted that a patch of sod, cut open by tool or toxin, slowly adds successive layers of organisms to recover itself, just as a wound heals over. This process begins immediately with microbes in the soil becoming active, he notes, growing exponentially into ever more evolved and complex natural systems, until balance is restored.

This intelligence of biotic life is largely ignored by modern people. But it's a magic and a marvel that was perceived and employed by ancient people. Ignoring it has enormous consequences. "Earth's remarkably stable atmosphere in a billion years is a sure sign of homeostasis—intervention of a self-correcting, self-stable intelligence," Yarrow notes.

From the microcosm to the macrocosm to Earth itself, stable systems are built upon intelligent actions, guided as much by faith and Spirit as by reason, to keep harmony and balance for all.

In my book, *Finding Sanctuary in Nature: Simple Ceremonies in the Native American Tradition for Healing Yourself and Others* (Findhorn Press, 2007) , I explain various ceremonies involving Earth energy that bring balance and harmony. One ceremony involves exposing raw soil, which can be a powerful step: when we consciously act to expose Earth and perform ceremony, we are operating in synchronicity with the Power of Earth to effect change. But, note also, as Yarrow points out, that this "uncovering" is not always by human intervention; it can be due to trauma or toxins or even natural causes, such as earthquakes, floods, droughts, or famines.

We may think we are the premier species walking upon Earth, but it is only an illusion. We define our sacred Nature by how we fit in, accommodate, adapt with, and promote the peace and harmony of Earth. Earth will always balance herself, with or without us. That should be a central tenet to the climate change debate: We can acknowledge our role in affecting the stasis of Earth, including agricultural practices, and do something about it, or we can accept the consequences—the extinction of humans and other species, for a while. It's a matter of scale. Earth lives in billions of years. The effects of humans on Earth are measured by far smaller units of measure.

Consider: 60 million years ago, humans were mammals the size of rodents, a morsel for meat-eating dinosaurs. Do you think that climate change for a few tens of thousands of years will make much of a difference to the life of Earth? While capable of making humans, polar bears, and other species extinct, shifts in geologic time have little bearing upon Gaia. It's urgent because it's urgent within our timeframe—and to us and all that we know of the world and rely upon. But to Earth, our imprint is relative.

Our role, as Native peoples understood, is to act with integrity within our scope for the next seven generations. If we each were guided by this fact, rather than adhering to the prevalent ideas of impermanence through modern culture, we can change not only Earth but ourselves for the better.

The Human Imprint:
Large in Human and Biological Events

While in the timeframe of Earth's lifespan human events are relatively short, the imprint of even small, collective action is large. A good example in relation to food and the environment is the impact of the Neolithic revolution of farming on who we are today and the world in which we live.

With the advent of farming came the possibility of providing abundant food to stabilize human populations, and as a result, they grew exponentially. But farming also changed the face of Earth and the peoples who inhabited the planet.

Evolution does not occur simply through changes in environment. Plants and animals themselves compete for resources and are always adapting to conditions, including those posed by each other (as in the case of the plants constantly shifting their chemical defenses against insects that want to eat them).

Even if the whole environment were stable, with no evolution, the plant and animal nations and individual plants and animals would continue to shift in their dance with each other and within their own species. This is why organics has it right—chemical applications are always short-sighted because plants and animals adapt, often quickly, and even more concerning, the ignored impacts of poisons in the environment and health effects are often long lasting as byproducts of the artificial inputs.

Scientists studying the DNA of humans can now see the impact of farming on human populations. Not only did farming create stable and rapidly growing communities, it also changed the biology of humankind.

In Asia, for example, the post–Ice Age descendants of "Negritoes," hunter-gatherers from Africa, were biologically overwhelmed by the burgeoning populations of Asian rice farmers. This is reflected, as well, in early European genes showing Near Eastern traits. Human populations shifted as a result of how food was produced. It's a global phenomenon, given the population growth that agriculture provided, and it all happened in a relatively brief 10,000 years.

But there's another dimension to this, as well. The change in diet changed populations, changed their genetics, and also produced biocultural change. Belief systems shifted along with these food and genetic changes.

Peter Bellwood created a firestorm with his book, *First Farmers: The Origins of Agricultural Societies* (Wiley-Blackwell, 2004), which upset the apple cart of the orthodoxy that Europe, existing as a continent unto itself, was somehow immune from the biocultural changes of the Neolithic revolution. The shift in food and human populations shifted the gene pool, as well as the culture. Increasingly, linguistic, genetic, and archaeological data show that cultures changed in more far-reaching ways than merely whether plants were wildcrafted by roving hunter-gatherers or intentionally planted.

Not only can environmental conditions bring about adaptations of plant and animal species but biological changes can spur evolutionary changes, too. In fact, it's a two-way street: a change in geographical conditions can spur biological and evolutionary changes, but biological and evolutionary changes can also spur geographical changes.

Remember Gilgamesh? He cut down the forests to build the cities and plant crops, but the resultant siltation made the water undrinkable, and the desertification destroyed the civilization he founded.

In his book, *The Last Hours of Ancient Sunlight: The Fate of the World and What We Can Do Before It's Too Late* (Broadway, 2004), Thom Hartmann recounts how the Paleolithic revolution brought down the last Mesopotamian empire, and unsustainable farming practices (eerily like those being promulgated by "scientific," "modern," and "conventional" farming) created the vast desert that exists today.

The demise of this empire cleared the way for the rise of Greece. But Greece also inherited the way of agriculture of the ancient Mesopotamians, denuding its forests for planting monocultures; its economy eventually collapsed, too, as the barren landscapes could only grow olive trees. Oversilted rivers, accumulated irrigation salts, and depleted soil failed to feed its population, and cities went into decline. That led to the rise of Rome, which followed the same agricultural practices that led to its decline, as well.

The pattern has been repeated since, with depletion in the Old World leading to exploration and conquest of the New World, until now, there is no more world to "conquer"—only our world that is left with unsustainable practices and headed toward global climate calamity.

The bottom line is this: The division between geographical or environmental evolution and adaptation and genetic and species evolution and adaptation is not a valid one. We are holographic in both how we react and what we choose to do, and our environment is part of that adaptive dynamic. The environment is not "out there," but right here—what you are doing with your hands and your heart and your mind. And neither can your hands be divorced from your heart or your mind without consequence.

Synergy and Unity of Purpose

The production of biochar as both a spiritual and practical activity by indigenous peoples of the Americas reflected a balanced synergistic relationship between humans and the environment. That unity of purpose and the resulting positive results were upended by the invasion of European settlers, who brought destructive, short-sighted patterns of development with them. It continues today, with the destruction of the rainforests in South America, as well as extractive practices elsewhere, creating an unsustainable and destructive hologram of its own.

As with any hologram, it changes as action changes. We may currently be in a situation that appears bleak globally regarding climate change and, indeed, unless human behavior changes, it is likely to worsen. But as we change our behavior, the situation changes, as well. In his outstanding book, *Eaarth*, Bill McKibben may have the facts on his side that it may be too late to return to the seasons and biologic milieu we once took for granted, that the carbon parts per billion in the atmosphere may be writing our future reality right now.

But that does not mean that collective action is for naught, or that individual action is meaningless. Indeed, as every great leader since well before Mahatma Gandhi has known, individuals have the power of choice on their side; a power that cannot be stopped by any institution, no matter how supposedly powerful or authoritative. As Jesus said, faith the size of a mustard seed can indeed move mountains. The power of human faith and action guided by Spirit can be transformative. Realities are nothing but interchangeable choices to immortal spiritual beings; even, and especially, in human bodies; in an infinite universe. Recognizing and employing spiritual power is the key to change.

From Jim's Farming Notebook: Start Small For Backyard Plot

In my organic column, I advise people to start small and to add to what they're doing. Rome wasn't built in a day, as they say.

Why not start with a 4-by-8-foot area, which we call in my column a "Jim's plot"? Or, if you already have one or two plots that size, why not add on to them in 4-by-8-foot increments?

To get it started, you can buy topsoil in bulk by the yard at some local yard and garden stores. For a 4-by-8-foot plot it doesn't take that much: for example, one cubic yard equals 27 cubic feet. It's mostly ground-up vegetative debris, so it's not going to be really fine or fertile. But it will fill up your bed. You'll only be using the top 5 inches or so of topsoil for most plants, so that's where you want to concentrate.

Don't feel like you have to actually fill the beds to the top. Start composting. When fall comes, rake and pile leaves for composting. Consider these beds as a beginning that you will add to over time, building up compost.

By the way: When you spread compost, only one-quarter inch on the top is needed when it comes to fertility; any more is overkill. As it adds layer upon layer, it will develop the way you want.

Till the ground in the beds and then add what you can, to a 4–5 inch depth. Rotate your beds. Plant, say, one or two 4-by-8-foot plots for a fall garden, and fill the others with leaves, cover them with black plastic over the winter and let them compost down.

That way, you'll have a deeper base to work from in the spring. A 4-by-8-foot "Jim's Plot" can put greens on your plate most of the winter (even at elevation in desert climates, if protected well with hoophouses), or tomatoes on the windowsill all summer, or herbs for seasoning anytime as a "kitchen garden." (You may find, in fact, that more of the people in your circles are interested in herbs by the ounce than produce by the pound and may earn much more per square foot taking that route.)

Our first garden after Annette and I got married was actually a driveway. We were living in a converted cobbler's shop with utterly no yard, in downtown Lena, Mississippi. Separating our house from the clinic next door was an old abandoned driveway belonging to the clinic. If you dug down an inch or so there was nothing but river rock gravel: chert. We worked out a deal with the clinic that if we could turn it into a garden, I would mow around the sides and back of the clinic; a deal they were happy to get because they had been paying for the service.

After working the ground, dumping compost and topsoil onto it, we grew a wonderfully abundant garden. But to be frank, I think it just grew on love.

After that, we moved to a place in the country, ShooFly Farm, where we have had 5 acres to play with.

Review

Postmodern organics, a new science for Earth:

- So-called "conventional" farming grew out of using war surplus chemicals, but the processes and methods, along with monocultural farming, are destroying the fertility of the soil and eradicating biodiversity. This "war" on food, and Earth, is unsustainable.
- The world can be seen as a far more interactive place by employing different perspectives, even scientifically, such as viewing a farm field in the infrared, which displays information that reveals the basis for plant-insect communication.
- Spiritual practices can work well with growing plants, enhancing the vibration rate of species for great health, nutrition, and abundance.
- Biocultural evolution occurs as a result of a culture's interaction with biology.

INTERNET KEY WORDS: *Fritz Haber, blackbody radiation, NPK, humus, tilth, One-Straw Revolution.*

CHAPTER THREE

The Bio-Cultural Choice:
An Edible Revolution

*To change something, build a new model
and make the existing obsolete.*

—*BUCKMINSTER FULLER*

We are at a crossroads. The dehumanizing of food, which includes its spiritual aspects, is having unintended consequences, including burgeoning populations with food allergies and obesity, greater scarcity of arable land from which to produce food, and ever fewer food species from which to derive nutrients.

It is a biocultural nightmare that began with the first significant biocultural revolution during the Paleolithic era: the introduction of agriculture. And it requires a new start, a second biocultural revolution, one involving new food choices that will allow us to re-envision agriculture as healthful and sustainable and, thereby, change our culture, our genetic makeup, and our world.

Huge and subtle shifts in how we view food and the individual's role in the food and agricultural system are taking place in the world. A growing interest in healthy, nutritious food and its production is reflected in the increasing consumer trend of organic food purchases. Gaining ground, too, is an emerging global agri-ecological movement, reflecting a move away from the entrenched and powerful food marketing system, with its reduction of "food" to processed "food products," toward a more direct and transparent relationship with food.

As Buckminster Fuller noted, the way to change something is to make it obsolete. Today's food giants and all they entail may seem overpowering, but change is happening everywhere. The great power of the subtle and fledgling food movement may be its myriad names and multitude of expressions. It includes moms vigilant about nutrition for their kids; public policy wonks zeroing in on obesity; food allergy specialists researching why our food is making us sick; farmers concerned about the natural fertility of their soils; "foodies" intent on novel, authentic dishes; the Slow Food movement celebrating authentic and heirloom foods; emerging countries' efforts to retain indigenous farming and not be swamped by industrial food imports; fair-trade shade-grown coffee plantations, and… well, you name it.

What is unfolding is the archetypal story of a relative handful of tyrants seeking to control our food supply, versus disparate voices calling for greater autonomy in something vital to them: in this case, their food, their health, and the health of the Earth community. In such a setting, the many small voices are far greater than the few large ones, as has occurred throughout history.

Syntropy Solutions

In his book, *The Power of Intention* (Hay House, 2004), Dr. Wayne Dyer talks about the power of creativity in resolving everyday challenges. He notes that careful observation and reexamination of commonly held assumptions can lead to wondrous innovation. For example, think about the first person to notice that ships don't have to be made of buoyant materials in order to float revolutionized shipping—in other words, that wooden ships didn't have to be wooden. It's the principle of displacement that allows steel ships, such as huge oil tankers filled with liquid, to float on water. And then there's the idea that something doesn't have to be buoyant in order to fly. Huge transport planes filled with heavy machinery or freight routinely fly around the globe and are anything but airy concepts, like balloons filled with helium.

Steiner noted the same principle in his Agriculture Course, that plants exhibit a quality opposite to gravity—of being pulled up, as well as being pulled down. This was before the invention of modern airliners.

Science has come up with any number of specific qualities of plants that seemingly defy Newtonian physics. One is a plant's turgor pressure, the force within a plant that allows it to grow through concrete. It's the observation of the thrust upwards that seemingly defies gravity that is relevant here.

The usual "scientific" or "logical" view of the world holds that Nature tends to move from order to disorder—the principle of entropy. Its opposite is syntropy, whose power lies in the fact that it is equal in its abilities. Syntropy is a natural phenomenon, as Steiner pointed out in his theory of biodynamics, but scientists today almost always ignore it. But the fact remains: focusing on uplifting, creation systems leads toward ever more complexity, or syntropy.

The word "syntropy" was coined by Albert Szent-Gyorgyi, a Hungarian scientist awarded the Nobel Prize in Physiology in 1937 for discovering Vitamin C. After moving to the United States at the end of World War II, Szent-Györgyi carried out pioneering work on muscle tissue and the dynamics of cancer. He identified two chemicals, one for growth and another for regression, but was stymied in finding a cancer cure. In his later years, he turned his focus to the dynamic principles often found in Nature.

With syntropy, Szent-Gyorgyi was attempting to refine a concept espoused by Erwin Schrödinger, a Nobel Prize–winning Austrian physicist who was one of the fathers of quantum mechanics. Schrodinger was convinced that negentropy, or negative entropy, (the concept Szent-yorgyi called syntropy) was the product of genetic code and present in everything. James D. Watson in his memoir, *DNA: the Secret of Life* (Alfred A. Knopf, 2003), credited Schrodinger's negentropy idea as the inspiration for him to research the gene, which led to the discovery of the DNA double helix structure for which he was awarded the Nobel Prize in Medicine in 1962.

The concept of syntropy, popularized by Buckminster Fuller, remains an attempt to unify the fields of biology and physics. Rudolf Steiner paved that road, in the vernacular of the day, defining the two opposing forces within Nature as physical forces (gravity) and Steiner's etheric forces (buoyancy). As with yin and yang, in any endeavor they are bound together. In fact, Szent-Gyorgyi said he gave up his attempt to cure cancer by researching the opposing chemicals he discovered because he could not isolate one from another until they had been expressed.

Entropy and Syntropy

So, how does one achieve the seemingly impossible task of overcoming the juggernaut that is the modern food/agriculture system through the use of syntropy? Easy—as Szent-Gyorgyi did: recognizing it and its opposite as essentially the same thing, and apprehending how one feeds the other.

The modern food empire is a perfect example of entropy. It is growing because it is fueled by artificial economics: cheap food subsidized by taxpayers. But it is doomed to fail because it's based on scarcity and lack: ruining the land it uses through dependency on dwindling fossil fuels.

Its opposite, syntropy, is the growing global movement toward sustainable, democratic systems that are healthy and empowering, and away from oligarchical top-heavy, imposed systems. "Arab Spring" and "Occupy Wall Street" are the same forces in reaction to governmental and social tyranny, where freedoms and resources are hoarded by the few at the expense of the many.

Simply choose another way: take responsibility for your own choices, including producing food or supporting the production of food in alternate ways. The rapidly advancing idea of urban farming and backyard gardening is one way to do this. Another is to support local food co-ops, to create food-buying clubs with friends and family, or start or sponsor community-supported agriculture (CSA) partnerships between small farms and consumers.

The creation of such local, self-supporting, intentional communities is a powerful avenue for change.[1] Similarly, citizens can hold politicians accountable for their votes in supporting farm legislation that shifts some of the taxpayer subsidies away from factory farms and the confined animal feeding operations (CAFOs) that are polluting the countryside. They can demand legislation that discourages monoculture "conventional" farming in order to promote better land-use policies—and promote legislation that helps farmers financially make the change to organic. They can insist on food labeling of genetically modified organism (GMO) ingredients, so that consumers can choose not to buy food "products" masquerading as real food.

Each of these is a step that can be taken to build community around shared ideals and ensure that voices being heard are those of voters, not just funders of political campaigns.

A Matter of Energy

How we relate to our food is important. Everything has energy and is affected by energy, so it's up to us how we define our energy usage. One way to define it is as the energy of oil refined to fuel, then used by minimum-wage farm hands driving a tractor across miles of farm fields growing genetically engineered plants, which are then harvested by combines, transported by truck, barge, or rail to giant grain facilities, and thence to processors that break them down into their constituent substances and into other chemicals to make food "products." Another way is to define it as the energy that people with loving hands bring to their work, as they gather food for themselves and others. In each case, it's the quality of energy that's different.

Missing from the discussion about the global movement toward food autonomy is an understanding of what *is* lacking: Spirit in our food. Just as governments tend to dehumanize political foes to motivate masses toward self-serving goals, so food has been neutralized spiritually to make its dehumanized production more palatable. Which would you rather purchase: a chemically sprayed, genetically modified clone of a nutritionally lacking but cosmetically perfect ear of corn that has never been touched by a human hand, or one that has been lovingly grown from seeds saved over generations? Shoppers generally choose the former because they have been conditioned to believe that's a better and safer choice, and to be suspicious of the latter as perhaps unclean, diseased, or less safe to eat.

This has led to the Snow White Syndrome. The apple is beautiful, perfect, but poisonous. What is hidden by the façade of that perfect apple is the fact that it has been drenched in chemicals, including serious poisons, and quite possibly covered in bug parts and rodent feces, as it is stored and transported thousands of miles, before being shrink-wrapped in off-gassing plastic for its display in the grocery store. Our cultural conditioning runs deep, and there is pressure for organic growers to present perfect produce—fresh-picked greens with a harmless bug hole or two are not easy to sell. Some blights, like the citrus canker, only affect fruits cosmetically, yet render the fruits completely unmarketable.

Food from your local farmer has been picked fresh only days or perhaps hours before, hand-washed by those who picked it, and probably also eaten by them and their families, too. Many conventional farmers grow their own organic produce for family consumption, eschewing what they grow for a living. There is no doubt that real foods that have been lovingly tended by people who care about the process from the ground up will taste better and be better for you. Again, it's a matter of energy.

The unique flavor of foods naturally grown, it has been argued, may not just come from their relatively high sugar content, or brix, but may be due to the chemicals the plant produces to repel insects and other threats. Food is a living entity; it is "in the process of being," not a "product." When people interact with their crops, they are working toward common goals of health, nutrition, and abundance. The fruit of that plant bears the result of all of those intents and prayers. When food is a product, it is an object—living in name only. It is no wonder industrial food lacks flavor.

Biocultural Evolution
Becomes Revolution

The biocultural process begins with choices: People choose which plants they wish to grow and which animals they wish to eat. That results in the selection of species that flourish. For example, few would recognize the grass with a large seedhead that grew in the mountains of Mexico and became the plant that now produces large ears of corn. Author and journalist Michael Pollan explores the mutual relationship of co-evolution between plant and human in his book *The Botany of Desire* (Random House, 2002), focusing on four plants: apples, tulips, marijuana, and potatoes. Humans cultivate them— the plants as we know them would not flourish without human choice—but the plants' evolution to adapt to human tastes, needs, appreciations, or longings also simultaneously cultivates the desire in appreciative humans to continue to spread the plants' genetic code. This is a form of biocultural evolution, whereby unconscious choices determine outcomes for the planet and for humans.

Culture shapes the way people think about their world and how they relate to it. The resulting choices can have powerful biological effects. These biocultural effects have been known to change the course of human evolution.

Biocultural changes are usually viewed from the standpoint of how humans and ecologies genetically adapt to one another. For example, lactose intolerance results from the lack of a digestive enzyme in some people that allows them to process milk or milk products. Primary lactose intolerance (the most common form) is called lactose nonpersistence. Most mammals become lactose intolerant after they are weaned, but those humans in the Paleolithic Revolution who domesticated animals for dairy products developed lactose persistence genetically so they could continue to consume dairy products into adulthood. Most people of Northern European descent have lactose persistence, whereas some African and Asian populations have adult lactose intolerance levels approaching 90 percent. This is a biocultural adaptation that began 10,000 years ago and continues today.

In another more ancient example of biocultural/biobehavioral features, one of the distinguishing characteristics of early hominid society was an increase in cultural interactions (learning/society), which changed the capacity of the brain and led to the development of larger frontal lobes. This, in turn, led to greater reasoning ability, more informed and creative food choices, and provided a more varied and healthier diet. This also coincided with more specialized and longer parenting, which imported more knowledge and adaptability to local ecologies. Culture provided knowledge that led to more and better food, which then resulted in more advanced societies and individual and family development. This positive example of biocultural evolution has had lasting impacts upon human development.

In a more modern example of possible biocultural evolution, food researchers have been watching ever-increasing numbers of people develop food allergies, particularly gluten or wheat insensitivity. While there is no scientific explanation, it's widely believed that consuming processed foods is the culprit.

Wheat has been considered the "staff of life" for much of the world since ancient times. So, how can this be? Until the mid-20th century, whole wheat was ground and all portions of it were used in making flour. Today, when a natural food such as wheat (or corn or soy) is processed, it is broken down into its "active ingredients." We are not eating the whole food, but pieces of it.

Refined wheat is created when the nutrient rich germ and the bran (the protecting coating rich in nutrients and fiber) are removed, leaving the endosperm (an edible part of the kernel containing starch and protein). The resulting "food" is poor in nutrients and even when "fortified" with vitamins is still far inferior to what the whole wheat would provide. In addition, chemical preservatives are added during food processing. Wheat proteins are used in a variety of products, including cosmetics, and it is now believed that these processed wheat proteins are often a contributing factor in allergies.

Culture also shapes the political economy, influencing which resources are made available. The recent cultural reaction against "Pink Slime," a beef industry processed food product is a case in point. In response to public outcry, the major suppliers of this dubious filler food product have filed for bankruptcy.

So, you are indeed making a "biocultural choice," when you choose foods that are healthy and demand that food products be labeled transparently, with any potentially harmful or questionable ingredients or sources clearly listed, including any processes or bioengineering involved. A culture that chooses mostly organic, pesticide-free foods, or products of eco-farming, would certainly have a positive biocultural effect.

When we make choices consciously, then, we trigger not merely biocultural evolution but biocultural revolution. That is, our food choices help change the course of human history mindfully, not as a result of market forces or mass-media conditioning.

When people take responsibility for what they put into their bodies, they are practicing biocultural revolution. When they choose organic foods, they are practicing biocultural revolution. When they insist that their governments label products truthfully and completely, they are practicing biocultural revolution. When they ban genetically modified organisms (GMOs) from agriculture and food, they are practicing biocultural revolution. When consumers choose to support small farmers, micro-farmers, and backyard farmers over "conventional" industrial agriculture and confined animal feeding operations that practice inhumane methods, they are practicing biocultural revolution. When people unite their spiritual and physical practices, or personal paths, such as yoga, with what they put into their bodies, they are practicing biocultural revolution. [2] When people join to create community-supported agriculture (CSAs) to provide food for their families, friends, churches, and society, they are practicing biocultural revolution. Their choices change society and culture and have a beneficial ecological and biological effect, creating a healthier, better society.

When they cause natural events to shift, humans are often making decisions with far-reaching implications without intending to do so. One example of harming the environment was when the pesticide DDT was used to kill insects in the 20th century; it almost made the bald eagle extinct. But on a more positive note, when gray wolves were reintroduced into Yellowstone National Park in 1995, scientists were astounded at the changes, far beyond simply reducing an out-of-control elk population. Since elk no longer lingered at streams, the water quality improved; fish populations increased; aspens and other trees flourished, as elk no longer ate the sprouts and, with greater cover and nesting habitat, bird populations increased; coyote populations dwindled, as wolves filled their predator niche, which increased animal diversity, including higher populations of pronghorn; beaver populations increased, creating more habitat for insects and migratory waterfowl; because wolves leave carrion from their kills, scavenger populations increased, including eagles, ravens, and bears.

Walking down the grocery aisle, most of us are perhaps unaware of how our food choices have impacted biodiversity on the planet, both in food and animal species. Pulitzer Prize–winning biologist Edward O. Wilson, who coined the term "biodiversity," observed that there are probably about one million trillion insects alive on Earth at any given moment. That sounds like an unassailable number, except when you consider that extinction of species is occurring at 10,000 times or more the rate prior to the rise of humans. Another way to look at it is that there has been no greater mass extinction on Earth for 65 million years, when the dinosaurs were wiped off the face of the planet.

In fact, some scientists have said that we should admit that this is the end of the Holocene Period and name the current epoch the Anthropocene ("anthropo" meaning human, and "cene" meaning new). *New York Times* writer Andrew Revkin got the ball rolling with his term Anthrocene in his book *Global Warming: Understanding the Forecast* (Abbeville Press, 1992), saying we ought to call this age something new, "After all, it is a geological age of our own making."

While the new geological period's start was suggested to be set at the beginning of the Industrial Revolution, others say that it more precisely began during the Neolithic Revolution: the beginning of farming. In fact, in arguing for this geologic view of humankind's impact upon Earth, and probably ending with the end of humankind itself, its characteristics include the amount of synthetic manures in disturbed soils, compaction of soils, pollutants in soils, soil erosion, and other ill effects from farming, grazing, and habitation. In other words, the staggering negative impacts humans are imposing on the globe through farming, industry, and overpopulation are continuing, accelerating, lasting, and in their depth and longevity may characterize a geologic age.

It's no longer a question of *whether* we are in the midst of a mass extinction but a question of *how fast* it is occurring: some estimates put the loss of species as high as 150 species per day. This massive dissolution of our ecology through man-made actions, or biocultural evolution toward the destruction of life on this planet, wasn't a conscious effort. It occurred, Wilson says, through a series of "small, largely unconscious actions."

As with syntropy being the negative entropy, we do not have to be victims of biocultural evolution; instead, we have to opportunity to act consciously in shaping culture to shift the environment. This is another example of how we create biocultural revolution.

The syntropy of this entropy is choice and mindful action. Consumers can choose to buy only foods that use no petroleum-based insecticides and herbicides, and that rely upon the sun to grow crops (natural fertilizers). They can buy locally from small farmers to bring the calorie of transportation per food item toward equality. They can choose to support only heirloom and natural seeds and growers of diverse food plants. Growers can practice seed saving and seed sharing, so that old lines are continued and diversity is maintained. [3]

And governments, with consumers as voters demanding it, can support the switch from "conventional" to organic or ecofarming, even permaculture, through tax incentives the same as industrial commodity farming is supported now. These are scalable actions—that is, the individual can effect these large changes by making small changes: through choosing brands, organizations, and politicians who support their views, and practicing informed, mindful choices in their daily lives.

A Community of Spirit

In an ideal situation, communities will arise in which individuals can pool their talents around the central theme of food and spirit as nourishing all. One example of a modern, eclectic community based upon an agricultural pursuit in which Spirit is a guiding force is the Findhorn Community in Scotland. Begun in 1962 by Peter and Eileen Caddy and Dorothy Maclean, it didn't start out as a spiritual community; it evolved that way.

As outlined in the book *The Findhorn Garden Story* (Findhorn Press, 2008) by the Findhorn Community, it started when Peter lost his job running a local hotel. They moved into a local trailer park (or caravan site) at Moray near the village of Findhorn. Feeding themselves and three children was a challenge, so Peter started trying to grow vegetables. Through intensive inner work, Dorothy discovered she was able to intuitively communicate with the spirit beings that tended the plants—a gift others quickly cultivated themselves—and the garden thrived.

People began coming from across the United Kingdom to learn how anyone could grow such bounteous crops of vegetables and vibrant flowers in the barren, rocky seaside shore in Scotland, including the now-legendary 40-pound cabbages that defied logic. The garden became famous.

From these humble beginnings, the community grew to encompass people of a spiritual nature from all walks of life. A program of learning, The Findhorn Foundation College, was established. The once-trailer park and environs grew into an internationally recognized ecovillage, described as being sustainable ecologically, economically, culturally, and spiritually and recognized by the United Nations as a Non-Governmental Organization (NGO) and able to participate in UN events. Around it, an array of businesses have sprung up that support its holistic approach.

It is important to note that there are many types of communities of Spirit: Buddhist or Christian monasteries, for example, or the kibbutz system in Israel, in which raising food is an integral part. A unique feature of the Findhorn Community is its eclectic nature and lack of written doctrine or creed. A spiritual community, as Findhorn suggests, does not have to be tied to a particular religion or belief system; the tenets are spirituality and sustainability.

In fact, Findhorn is a founding member of the Global Ecovillage Network, a nonprofit that links a diverse worldwide movement of autonomous ecovillages and related projects. There are intentional, mindful communities around the world that strive for a common vision. The impetus for Findhorn was connection with Spirit, or in Dorothy's case, ability to connect with the "overlighting" spirits of plants that she initially called angels, then *devas*, a Sanskrit word for "deity," generally interpreted as any benevolent supernatural being.

Types of Spiritual Beings

As more fully explored in my book, *Clearing: A Guide to Liberating Energies Trapped in Buildings and Lands* (Findhorn Press, 2006), there are any number of names for the invisible beings that co-inhabit Earth. Frequently encountered are elementals, the beings variously known by such names as sprites, fairies, and elves. Elementals attend to the earth's energies and manifestations, such as plants and water. Every culture has a name for them: faeries in the British Isles, "little people" among the Cherokee, *dryads* in Greece, *leshiye* in Russia, *shedim* among Jewish people, *afries* in Egypt, and *yowahoos* in Africa. Not all sprites, fairies, and elves are content with small chores; some are quite powerful spirits of the land.

Although such beings have been stereotyped in popular culture, they are actually quite diverse, in both appearance and function. In Ireland, for example, there are legends of the powerful Tuatha De Danaan, subjects of the Celtic goddess Danu. Although lumped under the category of fairies or elves, they are believed to be descendants of star beings who populated the earth ages ago and are, maybe not so coincidentally, similar in power and history to the beings ancient Tibetans described as the Lha. The Lha, according to a 13th-century account called the Chojung, came to earth when it was devoid of vegetation and manifested plants and animals through a form of deep meditation called *samten se,* which they eventually forgot how to do.

Most Native American cultures have similar legends about star beings (for more on star beings, see my book *Finding Sanctuary in Nature: Simple Ceremonies in the Native American Tradition for Healing Yourself and Others*, Findhorn Press, 2007). Even elves, which are often portrayed comically in popular culture, have a powerful pedigree. The name derives from the Scandinavian *alfar,* referring to "spirits of the mountains, forests, and waters."

Rudolf Steiner was primarily concerned with elementals, dryads, and undines. He gave seven lectures in which he went into great detail about his view of spiritual beings, outlined in the book *What is Biodynamics? A Way to Heal and Revitalize the Earth* (SteinerBooks, 2005). There is some general agreement about fey races among European followers, but they differ from source to source. Mainly that's because most ethereal beings, as described by Steiner and others, are first and foremost shapeshifters, and people's perceptions of them are colored by their own cultural upbringing.

In the general European way of viewing noncorporeal earth beings, the following definitions apply:

- **Nymphs:** Nymphs (for female, *nymphus* for male) and elementals overlap somewhat. Nymphs have a human shape. Elementals range from horrible-looking beings that feed off negative energy, often seen by alcoholics during delirium tremens, to amorphous shapes tending to flowers.
- **Dryads:** Dryads are beings that may have begun as nymphs but found that living in trees, or shapeshifting to resemble trees, or associating with certain types of trees, such as nymphs attending only to fruit trees (meliads), became their way of life and being.
- **Undines:** Undines is a broad term for water beings, which range from water sprites to mermaids and mermen. They often appear blue, and may have characteristics of water beings, such as gills, webbed appendages, or scales.
- **Sylphs:** Sylphs are beings of the air. Salamanders (not the amphibians of the same name) inhabit hot or arid areas. Trolls, gnomes, and "little people" are earth dwellers.

Nature spirits, large and small, are all around all the time, wherever on Earth we may be located.

But you don't have to "see" them to communicate with them. To perceive such beings, it's best when thinking of them to forget any preconceived notions and instead, trust what you sense or feel. *The Findhorn Garden Story* gives clear examples of communing with the Nature spirits of a place, purely intuitively. In it, Dorothy Maclean gives an account of her developing her "guidance," as she called it, describing it as engaging with God as an in-dwelling presence.

Drumming is a good way to enter nonordinary reality as part of the shamanic journey (see the step-by-step approach that follows at the end of this chapter). With training, one can learn to simply "apprehend" nonordinary reality, as outlined in my book *Dreams of the Reiki Shaman: Expanding Your Healing Power* (Findhorn Press, 2011).

Techniques such as employing Reiki or shamanic drumming to raise the vibration rate of a given piece of land can have profound effects. For example, one spring, a late frost came, so Annette went out to the garden and drummed to raise its vibration rate; other gardens succumbed to the freeze, but ours suffered little damage. Reiki Shamanism can be employed to speak with the spirits of the land directly, finding out what they desire, and helping to provide what's needed to grow more and better food.

Whichever way you decide to engage with Nature spirits, it is a natural process that, once a given technique is learned, gives value and meaning to the world in a way that has been previously unrevealed. It is a deeper way of being, a connection not only to Nature but to one's own natural self. It is quite simply a profound revelation to have the wool pulled from one's eyes and to truly see. By expanding ways of visioning, or cultivating inner knowing, seeing with your "Spirit eyes" allows you to expand your ability to create community by helping you tap into the pre-existing invisible community of plants, insects, and animals. It also connects modern communities with those in the past, such as the Essenes, Gnostics, and Native American societies, which lived in Spirit and created food and sought harmony.

In the teen years of the 20th century, Rudolf Steiner had the right idea, with his driving mission to reverse the dangerous course he saw civilization pursuing, one toward war, away from humanity, and away from Spirit.

His overriding goals were:

- To spiritualize the sciences.
- To make the earth hospitable to spiritual beings.
- To counteract threats to the earth and her produce.

However people or groups may align themselves with Spirit and natural growing methods, it's inevitable that from time to time crops will fail. The vicissitudes of Nature dictate winds that can blow down corn, or hail storms that will damage fruits and vegetables, or floods or droughts that will cause famine. These natural events have afflicted humankind since the birth of agriculture and have been the subject of great angst, soul searching, and even war, as societies seek essential resources to survive.

Sometimes, these events are seen as illustrative of a Divine intent, as in Exodus, with the 10 plagues of Egypt. Other times, as with the droughts in the American Southwest and in Russia of recent years, and the giant dust storms that have swept across China, they may be climatic cycles of long standing, perhaps exacerbated by shifting weather patterns, probably associated with climate change. They may indeed have a causative agent in the continuing imbalance of human activity polluting Earth with carbon-producing activities that no purely spiritual ritual can dispel. But certainly a spiritual solution is to recognize that Earth is a living ecosystem, and if humankind continues to ignore her needs, we doom ourselves, as well.

The risk of climate disruption can be mitigated somewhat by more sensitive agricultural practices. This includes eschewing monocultures, which lead to the loss of humus and living microorganisms that hold soil moisture and help to prevent erosion, desertification, and the loss of top soil that creates dust-bowl conditions. By planting trees and shifting farming practices toward a permaculture model, so that food-producing perennials are interspersed with annuals, we can create a more durable agricultural model for a changing climate.

Indeed, an argument can be made in favor of shifting toward a savanna model of planting. This involves planting more oxygen-producing and moisture retentive trees as "edges" around crop-producing open spaces, very much like the archetypal Garden of Eden (and the type of foodscape from which humankind sprang). This could be a better way to address the issue of agricultural resilience in a spiritual way, as the focus is not on blind ritual, or ceremonials, however heartfelt, but on the central position of any truly effective method of human interaction with Nature: mindfulness.

Humans are not victims of Nature; to view themselves as such denies the holistic nature of beings upon the planet—that all play a part. If humankind deals itself out of the equation by being mindless, unheeding, wasteful, and destructive, it will reap what it sows.

In the annals of spiritual interaction with Nature, the practices involving fearful savagery are the most hated and remembered, but that is because extreme weather conditions spurred fear and fear-based activities, such as human sacrifice and social upheaval. One might say that propitiating the gods was, in fact, feeding fear, with gruesome effect.

Human behavior hasn't changed. Fear begets fear-based responses, including today, perhaps, as reflected in the zeal of climate-change deniers. But that does not mean that spiritual solutions are ineffective, only that Nature can and does overcome any human behavior—even if it's creating sea rise because fossil fuel depletion raises the carbon level of the atmosphere that wipes out modern life. Gaia will survive—what's 65 million years in the heartbeat of Earth? Surviving species will then someday inherit the planet.

The charge to have dominion over the Earth and "subdue" it (Genesis 1:28) does not in any way imply wanton destruction, uncaring despoilation, or irretrievable desecration of Earth and its inhabitants. Humankind's challenge is to live in harmony with Earth and, thereby, coexist with other species and treat each other, including our earth, as ourselves.

Spirit alone, as understood and appealed to by humans, will not forestall natural disaster or weather disruption, but mindful behavior, based on spiritual principles and beliefs, will provide answers to any challenge. The challenge is to operate on faith, not fear, and with open hearts intent on communion and collaboration, not domination and control—the yin/yang of male/female views of looking at the world, again. The "old story" of dominion isn't working, says theologian Thomas Berry in his seminal *The Great Work: Our Way into the Future* (Broadway, 2000). We have a new story that is unfolding, one of respect for our earth and its beings. We live on a finite planet that we share with other beings, great and small. Plants and animals cannot exercise a conscience or restraint, so humans must, acting mindfully. This is the way of our salvation, as well as that of the beings with which we share this planet.

In Conclusion

We must decide our path: to forge forward with a new appreciation for food and spirit, or be overwhelmed by "Eaarth," as Bill McKibben calls it, a planet we cannot save and that is alien to us, where we are all subject to mechanization, industrialization, and corporatization of our most precious birthright—what we put into our bodies from the earth: our food.

As Steiner noted, intellects conditioned by an education focused on the material world cannot grasp the salutory effects of using spiritual practices for promoting agricultural growth. We must expand our vision and also look with our Spirit eyes, to acknowledge the invisible world that is integrated with the material one.

It's possible to realize Steiner's goals today. This postmodern approach to agriculture, which embraces Spirit, eco-agricultural and organic techniques, and employing science as a knowledge tool, is not an end in itself. Instead, it's a matter of returning balance to our outlook: in how we grow food, distribute food, and market and eat food.

By living holistically, seeing with our Spirit eyes, and joining others in our communities to make effective biocultural choices, we can raise our own Spirit food and bring edible prayers to the table.

■ From Jim's Farming Notebook:
Selling Your Crop

The major ways a market gardener can sell produce are:

- CSA
- Church groups
- Farm Stand
- Farmers Mark
- Restaurants, Stores

CSA

CSA stands for Community Supported Agriculture, whereby people buy a "share" in a farm's season and each week get a box of produce and/or fruit produced on the farm; or from ranchers, portions of beef, free-range chickens, or eggs, as they are available.

It works for the farmer, because CSA members contract up front, for 20 weeks or so, and hence the producers' high cost or "furnish" money is paid when it's needed, at the start of the growing season.

It works for the consumer, because the CSA member receives a mix of healthy, organic produce picked fresh and at a lower cost than normally found.

A couple of suggestions: First, a caution: I'm not sure that when you're just starting out that learning-by-doing is the best way to begin a CSA, per se, unless it is with family and really supportive friends who will forgive you if your crops don't pan out. Otherwise, folks who pay $400 or more for a season will expect a fair return and may not be so open-minded if plans go awry.

With that in mind, it might be best to consider your first year an experiment and allow for a learning curve (and lots of mistakes). Having neighbors chip in without a fixed pay schedule while you learn the ropes could do that.

Second, you might want to check with people operating CSAs and learn from their experiences, and ask them questions. It could be, if there are any in your area, they are looking to "go in with" others, even part time, to complete their offerings while you learn.

Third, there are some books you might want to read, first: Eliot Coleman's classic: *The New Organic Grower: A Master's Manual of Tools and Techniques for the Home and Market Gardener* (Chelsea Green, 1995); and, second, although a bit dated, it's chock full of practical advice and lessons learned the hard way: *Rebirth of the Small Family Farm* by Bob and Bonnie Gregson (Acres USA, 2004) Finally, for a general how-to that covers pretty much everything, there's *Backyard Market Gardening: The Entrepreneur's Guide to Selling What You Grow* by Andrew W. Lee (Good Earth Publications, 1992).

Some considerations: While it's a bargain to pay, say, $20 a week or so for fresh produce, for many people, that seems too high, when it adds up to $400 or more upfront to contract for a growing season.

Additionally, while, for the micro-farmer, a smaller subscriber list—say say 6–10 people—may be sustainable in terms of providing produce, variety may be lacking (for example, only radishes three weeks in a row or no tomatoes until later in the season). Transportation costs with farflung subscribers is an issue, too, as well as total income such as a small subscriber base provides.

To get around these issues, some CSAs in larger metro areas swap produce. Say, a person has a lot of tomatoes, while another has lots of carrots and yet another has mizuna. They might swap what they have in abundance for a more balanced box or bag on subscriber day.

Think about it. Your "Jim's plot" could be the start of a family or church CSA.

If you join with a couple of other church or family members, deciding who will grow what, you can feed a neighborhood or a congregation! For the elderly or ill, this could be a lifeline.

Farm Stand

Farm stands are usually employed by established market farmers—that is, folks who are well known in the community for growing and selling their goods. If you are located on a busy street or easily accessed area, it can pay off. But remember, too, that you must provide parking, keep your stand free of hazards, have insurance and certified scales for your produce (unless you sell by "the bunch," not by weight) along with keeping records for tax purposes. There's also the possible issue of a business license for the local community. It can be a big commitment, not the least of which is the cost involved in building the shed or stand. There also could be zoning laws or neighborhood covenants that must be considered. But for convenience for the farmer, if customers are available, there's no better way to sell produce. Some farmers just fill up the back of their pickup trucks and back it down the driveway abutting the road for their "stand." That can work, too.

Farmers Market

The most popular way to sell locally grown produce now—and a growing trend—is with farmers markets. State departments of agriculture normally keep a list of them. They are becoming quite popular. That is an advantage and a disadvantage, in that each has its own rules or "quirks," and some are more lax than others regarding what can be sold (such as produce only, or arts and crafts, too).

Something you might consider is joining with a few like-minded backyard growers and creating your own farmers market under the auspices of the state department of agriculture, if your local government allows it. Many small towns would love to have one to offer as an amenity for citizens, and as a tourism draw from surrounding communities, and might offer rent-free accommodations. Starting your own farmers market certified under the state offers sales tax and insurance protections that you would otherwise have to negotiate on your own; it also lends itself to allowing sales to those on food assistance.

Restaurants, Stores

Stores are great if they like organic produce for selling in bulk. That's why you are in business: to sell your produce. The downside is that you will be selling wholesale. Remember: Those $3/lb beans in the store you admire will only fetch you about 40 percent of that price when you haul in your buckets. That's often the hardest lesson beginning farmers must learn: wholesale pricing. At the store, corn may sell for four ears for $5 wrapped mighty prettily in shrink wrap, but the farmer may only get $9 a bushel!

Regarding restaurants, chefs are notoriously finicky when it comes to produce, especially organic produce. This suits the chef but can leave the farmer with lots of leftover and picked-over produce to sell.

It's really a meeting of minds from two different directions: chefs want the best produce that's available right now; farmers must think well in advance of what they want to grow and then plant the seed, wait for it to ripen, hoping for the best, and then sell what they have. The trick is to allow a way where both mindsets can flourish. For example, we've worked out with some chefs to meet with them at planting season and drop off a catalog, so that they can pick out what they might want.

Working out chefs' needs in advance can promote long-term relationships that are beneficial to both, and the discriminating diner! Also, we check with other growers and our retail organic outlets and see what others are growing, how much, and what the store's produce manager thinks customers will like. It doesn't make much sense to use up your limited space for turnips, for example, if you know another grower is going to plant acres of them.

You can make more money per item selling for a retail price at a farmers market, but another tradeoff is time. How much is it worth to you to spend all day waiting on customers that may never come? And are you willing to give what's left over to a food bank for free or throw it in the compost? A store might pay only a fraction of the sales price but you could sell your entire amount, with the store taking the risk of leftovers or spoilage, and you have your time free, as well. Each farmer must work out what works for him or her. It could be a mix of outlets, or just direct sales.

This is certainly not a definitive list or explanation of backyard market gardening, but it offers some suggestions to get started. Now, it's up to you to do it. Give it a try. The worst that can happen is that you waste some time and effort with a minimal amount of money (less than some hobbies like golf) and you might just earn some cash. That's in addition to providing healthful, nutritious food for you and your family. Enjoy!

Review

The biocultural choice, the edible revolution:

- As Buckminster Fuller noted, the way to change something is to make it obsolete, and the fledgling global food movement could change the course of more reliance on industrial farming toward a more caring way of providing food.
- Just as governments tend to dehumanize political foes to motivate masses toward self-serving goals, so food has been neutralized spiritually to make its dehumanized production more palatable.
- Culture shapes the way people think about their world and how they react to it and the resulting choices can have powerful biological effects. These biocultural effects have been known to change the course of human evolution.
- Choices made consciously become not merely biocultural evolution but biocultural revolution.
- The world is filled with spiritual beings; we must only learn to see them, or to allow them into our lives to help us.
- By joining with others in mindful actions, you can create communities of change.

INTERNET KEY WORDS: *syntropy, bioculturalism, dryads, faeries, little people, Findhorn community, intentional communities*

Accessing Nonordinary Reality

The steps for shamanic journeying are very simple. Most people begin to learn how to journey by traveling to the underworld to meet their power animal. The power animal is a being—actually, a power of the universe—that accompanies you wherever you go. We are each born with one to attend to us. Remember that fuzzy bear you carried around as a child? Or the unicorn? Or tiger? That was probably your power animal, or totem, from birth. We usually refer to power animals as animals, because animals are universal upon this planet and have recognizable qualities, such as bears and tigers being fierce protectors, while also furry and cuddly. However, the attending power can be anything, and they change through time. Although your totem may last throughout your lifetime, power animals come and go. Usually, you have at least one, though some people—shamans, particularly—can have whole menageries.

To begin, you will need to have a CD of drumming, or have a friend drum a steady beat for you, approximately 70 beats per minute. Any type of drum is fine, although a single-sided hand drum is easy to hold for long periods. Remo makes a wonderful synthetic drum called the Buffalo Drum, which is 16 inches in diameter, works well in all weathers, is inexpensive compared with hand-crafted leather drums, and travels well on airplanes. (For more information, as well as a CD for drumming, see the author's Web site: *www.blueskywaters.com*) A good first journey is 15 minutes. It may be useful to cover your eyes with a cloth to block out the light. Lie down, take a few deep breaths, and clear your mind. Imagine yourself in a cool, dark place, a waiting place, a good place to begin your journey. It could be a cave, or a place on a beach that you particularly enjoy. The main thing is that you want to have a hole nearby that you can go down into. Perhaps there is a tree with a bole in it in a park near your house. Or it could be a bridge that is dark underneath near your home. Some people even go down the kitchen drain!

After you have gained some proficiency at journeying, it is here where your power animal will come to greet you, at this waiting place, to take you above or below or outward into one of the three worlds. But this time, you want to go down the hole, whatever it may be, to meet your power animal. It could very well be that your power animal will show up now, even before you have entered the hole; it could be any type of animal, but you will recognize it for its friendliness; it will exude an aura of goodness—no sharp teeth or threatening manner-isms. It will also show you at least three different aspects of itself; for example, sideways, frontward, and backwards.

If your power animal shows itself to you in this waiting place, that's fine. Go with it, but if not, then imagine going down the hole you have chosen, going down, down, down, past roots of trees, through rocks (remember, you are in spirit form, you can go through anything, or around anything, or jump over anything—there is no limit to your powers, getting big or getting small, as the need arises). Keep going down, down, down, until you finally arrive somewhere. You will know you are there, because you will stop. Look around. It's likely you will see many power animals, and beings; or you may see none at all. Whatever you see, look at it for further reference later. But if there are many beings, remember that your power animal will show you itself in three different poses, and its energy will be one of connection and support.

Once your power animal connects with you, allow it to take you on a journey--hop on its back, or let it guide you as you fly. The sky isn't the limit; the horizons are limitless. After 15 minutes, have your friend drum you back, by doubling the tempo of the drum with the intent of energetically pulling you back into this reality. Your friend should say: "Okay, time to come back!" And you should wiggle your toes and stretch your fingers, allowing all your energy to come back into your body.

For more on the shamanic journey, as well as other ways to access nonordinary reality, see the author's book, *Dreams of the Reiki Shaman: Expanding Your Healing Power* (Findhorn Press, 2011).

Glossary

all-time, no-time. The present, accessed at its deepest level.

angels. Emissaries of light of Divine origin that accompany humans through life and are available for assistance and inspiration.

animus. The spark of life.

Anthropocene. A newly proposed geological epoch characterized by human impact upon the global environment.

anthropocentrism. The evaluating of reality exclusively in terms of human values.

apprehend. In the shamanic way of viewing, to take hold of, arrest, or seize, as perception in an act of understanding, in the moment, without judgment, or projection of consciousness.

archetypes. Attributes existing in potential form that can be brought into manifestation; original models after which other similar things are patterned.

ascension. Transcending to a higher level of consciousness; the next step in human and planetary evolution.

aura. Emanations of the energy body, often seen as colors that show moods, thoughts, or potentials; energetic fields surrounding the physical body, including physical, etheric, emotional, mental, astral, etheric template, celestial, and causal.

authentic self. Who you really are, not who you think you are, or have been told you are by outside sources.

biochar. A name for charcoal when used as a soil amendment, created by slow burning that captures carbon for plant use. When the first

Europeans came to the Americas, they found parklike forests and savannas that had been created by indigenous peoples using slow burning for biochar to fertilize the soil for crops, that with other amendments was essentially sustainable composting of soil for self-regeneration. This stewardship of the soil was centuries ahead of European crop science and possibly, if it had been adopted rather than stamped out, could have helped prevent current levels of carbon in the atmosphere and the severity of climate change.

biocultural evolution. Historical, evolutionary processes that occur as a result of a culture's interaction with biology.

biodynamic farming. Theory of growing plants that treats the farm as an organism that responds to the attentions of spiritual, elemental beings and employs special herbal and mineral preparations aligned with sidereal astrological events, based on the writings of Rudolf Steiner.

blackbody radiation. Coherent energy waves based on peak temperature of an object, which are unique to it, including weeds, trees, insects, and humans. As recorded, a great deal of information may be derived, including health and activities; can be used to judge health of plants and also psychological states of humans.

brix. Measure in plants to determine ripeness and other qualities. Light is refracted in juices by the quantity of dissolved solids, including natural sugars, vitamins, minerals, carbohydrates, enzymes, amino acids, nucleic acids, proteins, and other matter, which is measured by a refractometer and gauged as a brix scale measure of nutrient density and inherent health benefit.

centering. Locating the core of consciousness in the body; drawing magnetic energy from the earth and electrical energy from the sun to operate with balanced awareness.

chakra. Sanskrit for circle or wheel; in Indian Hindu thinking, the energetic centers in the core of the body linked by a central psychic energy channel.

cleansing. Transmuting energy to a higher, more positive form by raising its vibrational rate.

clearing. Dissipating (transmuting) negative energy. Clearing spaces usually also cleanses them since the act of clearing raises the vibrational rate.

co-creating. Operating as a partner with the Creator to boost positive energy.

deep ecology. Philosophy that recognizes the inherent worth of all living beings, not just in relation to the utility of them by human beings, recognizing that all living beings have the right to live and flourish. This essential indigenous belief runs counter to the "dominion" charge of Genesis, which many scholars now say must be changed. As Thomas Berry has said, a "new story" is needed now that recognizes the rights of all beings.

deep organics. Term coined by Eliot Coleman, a founder of the organic movement, to differentiate those who follow the spirit of organics from those who follow the letter of the more lenient USDA certified organic practices. In response to the perception that certified organics is being captured by industrial agriculture, as opposed to its small, local farmer roots, followers of deep organics are rejecting certification. Some also are turning to alternate certifying systems, such as Certified Naturally Grown, a grassroots alternative to certified organic for direct-market farmers and beekeepers.

eco-cosmology. Ecological worldview that shifts humankind's relationship in the cosmos from previous religious/philosophical man-centered formulas to a broader reverential universe; also called Green Tao. Eco-philosophy, of which eco-cosmology is a part, includes Ecosophy, The Deep Ecology Movement, New Christian Ecotheology, Ecology, Social Ecology and Eco-Feminism. For more treatment of these and other issues, see the Forum on Religion and Ecology at Yale, the largest international multi-religious project of its kind: http://fore.research.yale.edu/.

eco-farming. A form of sustainable agriculture with an emphasis on conservation and natural soil fertility and associated natural resource management systems that enhances productivity in harmony with ecosystems and biodiversity; often associated with eco-agriculture, which includes promoting rural livelihoods and/or fair trade, fair food principles for producers, especially in global trade, indigenous peoples.

ego. The survival mechanism, which is part of the personality. See personality.

energy. Subtle power manifested through life force, frequency, or cohesion.

energy body. A body that exists beyond the physical plane; in humans, such a body extends 27 feet in each direction, and thereafter continues into other dimensions. See aura.

entropy. The tendency of disintegration of any form of organization. See syntropy.

Essenes. A sect of Judaism that flourished from the second century BCE to the first century BCE. Given the words attributed to Jesus, as the Dead Sea Scrolls reveal, he either was an Essene or was deeply influenced by them. The group was heavily invested in what would today be called esoteric beliefs, and had a close affinity with angels in the conduct of daily life.

Eutrophication. The effect of excess nutrients, such as fertilizers or sewage, on a body of water. This is a condition mainly caused by agricultural run-off. The changes caused by eutrophication are myriad disruptions of the ecosystem, most of them harmful.

Fair Trade. A trading partnership, based on dialogue, transparency, and respect, that seeks greater equity in international trade and that contributes to sustainable development by offering better trading conditions to, and securing the rights of, marginalized producers and workers.

fast. See vision quest.

flow of creation. The movement or stasis of energy in a given moment.

Gaia theory. The belief that Earth has a consciousness of its own; Earth known as Gaia.

GMO. Stands for "genetically modified organisms," generally referring to any product of genetically engineering, which may include crops and food products made from GMO plants, including transgenic organisms that have DNA inserted from different species. GMO seeds and plants are specifically banned from certified organic crops and foods. Most modern nations, with the exception of the United States, at least require labeling of foods that include GMO ingredients.

Gnostics. A branch of Judaism and early Christianity that flourished during the second and third centuries AD, until crushed as heretical by Rome. Its followers are believed to have included some disciples and relatives of Jesus. It was marked by open-mindedness and a view toward equality of women (including women as disciples and leaders of the church) that went against the more tightly structured and male-dominated Rome-backed church.

God vs. Creator. God is one, all; the Creator is the active aspect of God as expressed in the will of creation.

goddesses. Land spirits of the highest order, usually associated with a place or characteristic; also, humans who have transcended but chosen to remain on Earth in spirit form as a means of service.

grounding. Connecting with the earth energetically to ensure that consciousness is not operating from other dimensions or overly affected by other energetic forces.

guides. Spirit helpers, soul brothers or sisters from former or future lifetimes, or spiritual masters who have assumed a supportive role for a particular soul's evolution.

healing. Bringing to harmony and balance, wholeness.

heartsong, or **power song.** A song that expresses the unique, positive energies, traits, and intents of an individual, usually discovered through fasting and prayer.

higher power. God as expressed through one's highest Nature.

life-force energy. Energy that is all around us in Nature and that is emitted by the earth.

light body. Energetic body; the quality of energy around a person, as opposed to their physical body. See MerKaBa.

matter. Patterns of energy we perceive as having substance.

medicine. The inherent power within all things.

medicine wheel. A Native American system of prayer, meditation, and discovery, recognizing that life follows a circle. The wheel's directions and their significance, concepts from which all things are said to derive, include east (newness, discovery), south (youth, growth, healing), west (introspection, setting sun, light within), north (wisdom, elders, ancestors), center (soul, spirit), above (Heavenly Father), and below (Earth Mother).

meridians. Lines along the body where energy is channeled; often used in acupuncture and other energy medicine to effect healing.

MerKaBa. In sacred geometry, a star tetrahedron; an energetic framework that forms a blueprint for spirit to attach to and from which, in plants and animals, DNA creates a physical expression; a geometric form that includes the light body; a pattern of energy shared by animals, plants, stones, and all objects, including those that are man-made.

mind of God. Expansion of human thought to higher consciousness as far as is conceivable.

monoculture. It's a startling fact that only about 4 percent of the varieties of vegetables available for planting at the beginning of the 20th century still exist today. It's equally astounding that only three grain crops—rice, wheat, and corn—make up more than half of all the food consumed globally. That's even more striking when it's considered that in the North American continent alone, indigenous peoples chose from up to 5,000 different species of food plants prior to European discovery. This narrowing of food plant choices is further exacerbated by GMO seed makers buying up seed companies and discontinuing lines of seeds in favor of selling their patented engineered seeds. And it has had a decimating effect on soils and the natural fungi, insects, and other life that live outside the sterile monocultures of modern, chemical "conventional" farming.

morphogenic field. A universal field encoding the basic pattern of an object. From the Greek *morphe,* which means "form," and *genesis,* which means "coming into being." Noncorporeal beings manifest in three-dimensional reality through morphogenic resonance.

native peoples. Indigenous cultures practicing traditional Nature-based ways.

nonordinary reality. Reality as seen when everyday constraints and predispositions are eliminated through trance or other methods.

NPK. Symbols for nitrogen, phosphorus, and potassium found on fertilizer bags, often wrongly believed to be the only elements necessary for proper plant growth. Trace elements are essential for nutrition in plants and animals.

organic farming. A form of agriculture that utilizes the principles of crop rotation, green manure, compost and other natural fertilizers, and nonsynthetic means, including biological pest control to promote plant growth and soil fertility (using certified organic or heirloom seeds and excluding hybrid and/or genetically modified seeds).

overlays. Theory that reality is composed of layers and may at any time be changed, even radically, by simple actions.

timelines. Theory that realities extend from points in time, creating histories from point to point.

permaculture. Sustainable land-use design based on natural ecology of land and plants, using biological principles found in the patterns of Nature.

personality. All that we adhere to, or believe, that makes us who we think we are. See ego.

portal. A vortex through which objects and entities can pass from one dimension of reality to another while realm shifting.

power animal. An animal that offers guidance and protection; a totem.

power song, or **heartsong.** A song that expresses the unique, positive energies, traits, and intents of an individual, usually discovered through fasting and prayer.

power spot. A place where all energies of a structure or tract of land are focused.

prana. Universal life-force energy.

quorum sensing. A process by which bacteria communicate with each other to behave as a collective population.

Reiki. A Japanese form of energy medicine involving sacred symbols and guides; use of the hands to channel healing energy.

sacred circle. All beings in our lives—past, present, and future—who are connected to us; consecrated circle for ceremony.

sacred geometry. Symbolic and sacred meanings found in specific geometric shapes, relationships between objects and geometric proportions.

self-talk. The inner dialogue inside our minds; it can be positive, as in life-affirming, which promotes inner peace and harmony, but may also include negative self-talk: the "what ifs," "buts," judgments, and fears that prevent us from being who we really are.

shaman. Siberian word meaning "one who sees in the dark"; a person who uses earth energy, guides, and power animals for insight; a medicine man or woman.

shielding. Creating, through intent, a protective energy layer around you to deflect external negative energy.

shift of the ages. Powerful changes in energy patterns now occurring on Earth as a prelude to Earth transformations and humanity's eventual development of higher consciousness.

smudging. Burning a plant such as sage, cedar, or sweetgrass to purify the energy of an area; can include sacred formulas in liquid form for clearing.

Snow White syndrome. Refers to the beautiful, perfect poison apple in the Snow White fairy tale. Factory farmed, conventionally grown produce is like the poison apple; it is perfect, but can be laden with poisonous pesticides, herbicides, and other chemicals.

soil testing. Having agencies test soil to determine which elements may be missing that are necessary for healthy growth.

soul. The essential life force, or essence, of a being that is eternal from lifetime to lifetime.

soul retrieval. The act of retrieving soul parts, or essence, lost through trauma or stolen by another individual.

space. Any defined area, including the objects within it.

spiral of ascension. Spiral of life that offers a changing perspective as new lessons are encountered and old ones repeated, until the lessons are finally learned.

spirit. The essential quality of a being as an expression of soul; noncorporeal aspect of a person aligned with their soul purpose.

spirit quest. Following only what spirit dictates, usually over the course of days.

stillpoint. An inner place of total silence and stillness, where intuition and creativity originate and balance can be found; the source of being.

sustainability. The term has been used so broadly and variously that today it is almost a word without meaning. But in general, sustainability entails acting in accordance with an objective understanding of the interconnections among environmental, social, and economic needs—the practices of living within present means and distributing resources and opportunities equitably, in order to preserve and enhance quality of all life for future generations. A shortened version is often used: Meeting current needs without sacrificing the ability of future generations to meet their own needs. Note: to be ethically conscientious, it should include all beings, not only human beings.

synchronicity. A term coined by the Swiss psychiatrist Carl Gustav Jung (1875–1961) defining a meaningful acausal coincidence of a psychological event and an external observable event, both taking place at, or around, the same time; a coincidence with meaning, seemingly beyond statistical happenstance but without a provable link.

syntropy. The process evolving from chaos to ever more sophisticated orders of development, or negative entropy. See entropy.

thought forms. Organized patterns of energy, either free floating or embedded in a space, that can be broken up by rattling or other means of transmutation.

tilth. Positive condition of soil from humus and other byproducts of living matter that create tiny air pockets or loft, leading to a crumbly texture that promotes growth.

transmutation. Changing energy from one state to another, such as transforming water to ice or vapor, and vice versa; changing negative, or inert, energy into positive, or active, energy; or neutralizing energy to be reabsorbed by the earth. Ancient practices involved burying an energized object in the ground, burning it with fire, or submerging it in water.

umane. (*OO-mah-ne*) Lakota word for a sacred symbol of Earth energy in its raw form, often depicted in stone pictographs as a square with lines of energy from each corner, or as a square with enlongated corners to represent power coming from and going out to all corners of the universe.

unoli (*you-know-lee*). Cherokee word, literally meaning "winds," used as a designation for the powers of the directions.

vibrational rate/vibrational frequency. The measurable level of energy of a person, place, or object; the higher the rate, the closer to the source, or optimal wholeness.

vision quest. A period of time spent in a desolate or isolated spot under the tutelage of a spiritual elder, intended as an opportunity for discovering the inner self, the meaning of life, or to connect with higher beings.

vortexes. Doorways, or portals, into other dimensions; areas where energy in flux can affect time and space.

wild spirit. A spirit of the land that usually inhabits wilderness areas away from civilization or contact with humans; ally.

will of creation. Energy of the moment, moving from one state to another; the potential to transform to another manifestation.

Resources

If you haven't set up a Twitter account, I'd recommend it for a quick easy "take" on what's happening in the world each day. Politicians, world leaders, celebrities, and interest groups of every kind now use it to announce their doings, often well before traditional media can get around to reporting it, and you can, too!

For example, when we're in harvest season at ShooFly Farm, I announce my deliveries; just a simple note, like: "Just delivered fresh #organic kale to Rainbow Whole Foods." That message goes out to all those who follow our Twitter account. I know it works, because the produce manager says every time I "tweet," people come in asking, "Where's the ShooFly produce?"

By the way, the hashtag (#) used with Twitter is a shorthand version of keywords, so that anybody who wants to know what's happening regarding organic issues can just put "#organic" in the search box, and anything regarding organic that's been posted anywhere pops up. You can also use Twitter to advertise yourself or your product. While it's true that 140 characters is not a great amount of space to tout one's virtues or interests, with a little thought, you can do it. Consider it a haiku of you!

For example, while I was writing this book, I put as my intro on Twitter:

Jim PathFinder Ewing

@EdiblePrayers #Journalist #author Look for Jim's new book, Conscious #Food: Sustainable Growing, #Spiritual #Eating (Findhorn Press) this fall. #mindfulness #wellness

#eco

It's not eloquent, but it gets the point across.

Try Twitter. It's free. It's easy. But, look out, it can be addicting! I try not to spend more than a few minutes each day on it. But with a smartphone, one can be in constant touch with anyone.

Here's a list of useful Twitter addresses for people who comment on food, agriculture, organics, or spirit. It is, of course, by no means definitive, but these "tweeters" frequently provide links to news, articles, blogs, webpages, events, and information that is timely. Please note, spelling, punctuation and descriptions are those used by the individual tweeter. For more information on Twitter, I have two accounts that I keep updated:

— **@OrganicWriter**, which has information on food, organics, and agriculture; and

— **@EdiblePrayers**, which has information on health, wellness, spirit, the environment, and other issues. @EdiblePrayers has more lists of other tweeters on these subjects and others.

Other Twitter resources, in no special order:

- **Guardian Environment @guardianeco.** Green news, comment, and more, run by the environmentguardian.co.uk team.
- **Lisa Baertlein @LisaBaertlein.** Reuters correspondent on the food beat. Views are my own and links are not endorsements.
- **Lisa Hymas @lisahymas.** Lisa Hymas is senior editor at green news site *Grist.org*.
- **Grit Magazine @GritMagazine**. Celebrating country lifestyles, while emphasizing the importance of community and stewardship
- **Econundrums @Econundrums.** Weekly *Mother Jones* column that answers thorny environmental questions.
- **utne_altwire @utne_altwire**. The Best of *Utne Reader's* alternative sources (and the sources they follow) in a socially curated magazine from the real-time web.

- **Cert Naturally Grown @CNGfarming**. The grassroots alternative to certified organic for direct-market farmers and beekeepers.
- **Just Label It @justlabelit.** We have the right to know what's in our food. Visit our website to tell the FDA to Just Label It. Tweets/RT/Follows ≠ endorsements.
- **Food+Tech Connect @foodtechconnect**. We connect innovators at the intersection of food and tech through news+analysis, events, and strategy consulting.
- **Bryan Welch @ranchocapp**. Media exec (*Mother Earth News, Utne*, and so on), Farmer, Conservationist, and Author of *Beautiful and Abundant: Building the World We Want*, *www.beautifulandabundant.com.*
- **Monica Eng @monicaeng**. I'm a writer who covers health, food policy, cooking, and sustainability for the *Chicago Tribune*.
- **Helena Bottemiller @hbottemiller**. Politico, food/ag policy geek, reporter for *Food Safety News.*
- **Young Farmers @NYFCNYFC**. The National Young Farmers' Coalition is a new organization created by and for the next generation of family farmers in the United States.
- **Gail Wadsworth @GailWadsworth**. Food activist and locavore executive director California Institute for Rural Studies.
- **OWS Food Justice @FoodJusticeOWS**. Twitter account of the Occupy Wall Street Food Justice working group.
- **Edible Communities @ediblestories**. 2011 James Beard Award winners for Publication of the Year. 65+ regional food magazines across the US and Canada.
- **Mother Earth News @MotherEarthNews**. The Original Guide to Living Wisely: Organic Gardening, Homesteading, Renewable Energy, Sustainable Food and Farming, DIY, Green Homes, Natural Health and More.

- **Acres U.S.A. @AcresUSA.** Acres U.S.A. is the leading publisher for commercial-scale organic and sustainable farming.
- **Crop Diversity Trust @CropTrust**. Our mission is to ensure the conservation and availability of crop diversity for food security worldwide.
- **changeEnviro @changeEnviro**. Change.org is the world's fastest growing platform for social change. Here you'll find all the latest news and campaigns about environmental and climate issues.
- **John Stauber @jcstauber**. Agitator, Instigator, Author of Toxic Sludge Is Good for You; Weapons of Mass Deception; etc. Founded Center for Media and Democracy in 1993, ran it until '09.
- **Seedstock @Seedstock.** Seedstock is the blog for sustainable agriculture focusing on startups, entrepreneurship, technology, urban agriculture, news, and research.
- **NYT Green Blog @nytimesgreen**. A Blog About Energy and the Environment from The *New York Times*
- **greenhorns @greenhorns**. Working nationally to promote, recruit, and support young farmers. Events! Film! Radio! Blog! Wiki resources!
- **EIN Food Safety News @EINFoodSafety**. Latest food safety news for business professionals and analysts. Food Safety News Today is a media monitoring service provided by EIN News.
- **AGA @aga**. The American Grassfed Association promotes grass-fed livestock producers and products through communication, education, research and marketing.
- **House Ag Committee @HouseAgNews**. News and updates from Chairman Frank Lucas (OK-3) and the House Agriculture Committee.
- **AGree @AgreeAgPolicy**. Bold, new initiative designed to tackle long-term agricultural, food, and rural policy issues.

- **Yobo @yourolivebranch**. A nonprofit that shares positive news stories from both its readers and traditional news outlets in order to help further global peace and sustainability.
- **Judy Walker @JudyWalkerTP**. Judy Walker is food editor at *The Times-Picayune*.
- **Rodale News @RodaleNews**. Your trusted news source for healthy living on a healthy planet.
- **Grist @grist**. Environmental journalism at its best. A beacon in the smog, if you will. Tweets by *Grist's* social media producer, Hanna Welch.
- **Hank Will @HankWill**. Farmer; Gardener; Reader; Thinker; Scientist; Editor in Chief, *GRIT* Magazine
- **Sara Sciammacco @EWGFoodNews.** EWG press secretary focused on agricultural and food policy, farm subsidies, nutrition, conservation, pollution, pesticides, bottled water, and biofuels.
- **Non-GMO Project @NonGMOProject**. An informed choice for North Americans who want to avoid GMOs in their food and products.
- **Connected Roots @ConnectedRoots.** Connected Roots is a project to help urban people grow more for themselves and then share what they grow with others. Social, Cheap, Fresh.
- **Philip Brasher @PhilipBrasher.** Editor, Executive Briefing - Agriculture and Food, CQ Roll Call, part of *The Economist* Group.
- **Robyn O'Brien @unhealthytruth**. A former food industry analyst, I traded a briefcase for a diaper bag, had 4 kids, wrote a book, gave a TEDx talk on health, & founded the AllergyKids Foundation.
- **Mark Bittman @bittman**. Writer on food for *New York Times* Opinion and Magazine, and others. Author of *Food Matters* and *How to Cook Everything*. See also: http://markbittman.com.

- **Marion Nestle @marionnestle**. Paulette Goddard Professor in the Department of Nutrition, Food Studies, and Public Health.
- **Naomi Starkman @NaomiStarkman**. Good Food Advocate. Food Policy Consultant. Co-Founder/Editor-in-Chief, *CivilEats.com*.
- **Tom Philpott @tomphilpott**. *Mother Jones*; Maverick Farms
- **Rodale Institute @RodaleInstitute**. Organic pioneers since 1947. Through organic leadership we improve the health and well-being of people and the planet.
- **Peter Kobel @TheEcoist**. Writer, author, advocate for environmental, economic, and social justice.
- **GMWatch @GMWatch**. Countering the propaganda of the biotech industry.
- **NEBeginningFarmer @BeginningFarms**. Cornell Small Farms Program tweets farmers, farm technology, and news, agriculture, urban farms, extension, farm life, ag ed.
- **Amer. Farmland Trust @Farmland**. American Farmland Trust - We love Farmland Protection, Local Food, Farmers Markets, Family Farms, Farmers, Sustainable Ag., and Farming in General…
- **FairFoodFight @FairFoodFight.** A blog and social media site connecting people who give a crap about local, organic, and real food. And Mexican wrestling. A project of Equal Exchange Co-op.
- **EcoFarm @Eco_Farm.** Promotes ecological agriculture through education, alliance building, and advocacy.
- **Michael Pollan @michaelpollan**. Author of *Food Rules; In Defense of Food; The Omnivore's Dilemma; The Botany of Desire; A Place of My Own;* and *Second Nature.*
- **Organic Nation.tv @OrganicNation**. Exploring America's sustainable food landscape.
- **Food Alliance @foodalliance**. Most credible and comprehensive certification for sustainable food in North America.

- **NSAC @sustainableag**. National Sustainable Agriculture Coalition (NSAC) on federal ag policy. Working for family farms, the environment, healthy food, strong communities!
- **Danielle Nierenberg @NourishPlanet**. We highlight environmentally sustainable ways of alleviating hunger and poverty. Innovation to share? Visit: NourishingthePlanet.org
- **Paula Crossfield @civileater**. Managing editor of *Civil Eats*, *Huffpo* blogger, contributing producer at *The Leonard Lopate Show*, rookie gardener, avid cook, food policy wonkette.
- **Organic Consumers @OrganicConsumer**. Campaigning for health, justice, sustainability, peace, and democracy!
- **OFRF @OFRF**. To foster the improvement and widespread adoption of organic farming systems.
- **OSA @Seed_Alliance**. Organic Seed Alliance advances the ethical development and stewardship of the genetic resources of agricultural seed.
- **Food Declaration @RootsofChange**. Working to ensure every aspect of our food—from the time it's grown to the time it's eaten—can be healthy, safe, profitable, affordable, and fair.
- **Organic Trade @OrganicTrade**. OTA is the membership-based business association for organic agriculture and products in North America.
- **food_democracy @food_democracy**. Dave, Founder and Director of Food Democracy Now! Creating a sustainable future through positive food and farm policies.
- **Johnny's Seeds @JohnnySeeds.** Johnny's Selected Seeds is committed to helping growers and gardeners succeed with superior seeds, tools, information, and service.
- **Seeds of Change @SeedsofChange**. Official home of Seeds of Change on Twitter. We offer Certified Organic Seed and Food products that are good for you and the environment.

- **Slow Food USA @SlowFoodUSA**. Building a good, clean, and fair food system.
- **Civil Eats @CivilEats**. A site that promotes critical thought about sustainable agriculture and food systems as part of building economically and socially just communities.
- **350 dot org @350**. Join a global movement that's inspiring the world to rise to the challenge of the climate crisis. 350=safe upper limit of CO_2 in atmosphere.
- **Waylon Lewis @elephantjournal**.
- **seedliving.com @SeedLiving**.Tweeting about seeds, bees, homesteading, permaculture, biodiversity. Buy, sell, swap homegrown products.
- **Quaker Farm @QuakerFarm**. Sustainable living because it matters. Cotswold sheep, Raw Honey, Bakery, Collie dogs, workshops. Online children's photo stories about farm life. Michigan.
- **Don Carr @DonEWG**. Senior Advisor at the Environmental Working Group.
- **Jones Farms Organics @JonesOrganics** We live in the majestic San Luis Valley in Colorado and grow organic, nutrient dense potatoes, hay, grain, and grassfed beef.
- **CA Farmers' Markets @CaFarmersMkts**. California Farmers' Markets Association, where you buy fresh produce direct from the farmer. Local, organic, farm fresh every day!
- **bayareabites @bayareabites**. Bay Area Bites is KQED public media's food blog.
- **MA'O Organic Farms @maoorganicfarms**. MA'O is a Hawaiian social enterprise growing organic food and young leaders working for a sustainable Hawaii.
- **twilight greenaway @twyspy**. Food editor at *Grist.org*. Also a lover of strange and unexpected things in all categories. (note: I am NOT a fan of the vampire movies).

- **Franke James @frankejames**. Artist and author of *Bothered By My Green Conscience* | *Who cares about the Forest?* | *Six Tools for Climate Change* Art + more...
- **HavenBourque @HavenBourque**.Communications strategies for food, environment, and community. *CivilEats.com* blogger. Social media evangelist. Loves coffee, and food access myth busting.
- **Seed Matters @Seed_Matters**. Seed Matters advocates for the improvement and protection of organic seed to ensure healthy, nutritious and productive crops for people, now and in the future.
- **CoFED @TheCoFed**. We empower communities of students across North America to create financially sustainable campus hubs for food and social justice activism.
- **GMO Journal @GMOjournal**. Exploring the debate concerning genetically modified organisms, crops, and foods. If you are what you eat, then aren't you a GMO?
- **Max Goldberg @livingmaxwell**. Organic food is my passion. I blog and tweet about all things organic food: products, news, trends, and legislation. Love meditation, been doing it since 1991.
- **Organic Valley @OrganicValley**. Organic farm cooperative producing milk, cheese, butter, yogurt, eggs, soy, and juice. Keeping farmers on their land since 1988.
- **Raw Milk Colorado @RawMilkColorado**. Raw Milk Association of Colorado (RMAC) advocates traditional raw milk products and seeks to ensure a safe supply. Producers, Consumers, Locavores, Free to choose.
- **helpthebees @helpthebees**. Raising awareness of the plight of bees and what we can do about it. Wildlife lover, enjoy wildlife gardening and interested in environmental issues.

- **Cornucopia Institute @Cornucopia_Inst.** Promoting Economic Justice For Family Scale Farming And Organic Foods.
- **wendy wasserman @wendywas.**
- **My Organic Footprint @Organic_InfoHub**. Increasing My Organic Footprint. All things organic including farming, gardening, lifestyle, products, restoration, trade and research.
- **OrganicSchoolProject @OrganicSchool**. The Organic School Project is a non-profit that seeks to reconnect children with their food source by improving the way schools serve lunch.
- **Bob Weisenberg @BobWeisenberg**. Associate Publisher, *elephant journal* * *Yoga Demystified* http://bit.ly/mVa3NH * *Bhagavad Gita in a Nutshell* http://bit.ly/eMXaRF
- **Geoff Garver @gginmont.** Working to build a whole earth economy.
- **Doug Barasch @DougBarasch**. Editor-in-Chief, *OnEarth* Magazine.
- **Leopold Foundation @AldoLeopoldFdn**. Fostering the land ethic through the legacy of Aldo Leopold by enhancing understanding and love of land.
- **NYTimes DotEarth @dotearth**. NYTimes.com/DotEarth is Andrew C. Revkin on Climate Change and Sustainable Living.
- **EarthIslandInstitute @earthisland**. Earth Island Institute grows environmental leadership to support the biological and cultural diversity that sustain the environment.
- **EarthPolicyInstitute @EarthPolicy**. Dedicated to planning a sustainable future as well as providing a roadmap of how to get from here to there.
- **Whole Planet Tweets @WholePlanet**. Whole Planet Foundation is a nonprofit organization established by Whole Foods Market that provides grants to microfinance institutions around the globe.

- **Ecotrust @Ecotrust**. Innovate, invest, and inspire in ways that create economic opportunity, social equity, and environmental well-being.
- **IATP @IATP**. IATP works locally and globally at the intersection of policy and practice to ensure fair and sustainable food, farm, and trade systems.
- **@Nature_org.** The Nature Conservancy welcomes you to its official Twitter site! We're a leading conservation organization working for people and Nature.
- **Rainforest Alliance@RnfrstAlliance**. International nonprofit organization working to conserve biodiversity and ensure sustainable livelihoods
- **Worldwatch Institute @WorldwatchInst**. Global environmental research organization focused on building a low-carbon energy system, creating a healthy future for agriculture, and developing a green eco.
- **Earth Charter @earthcharter**. "The Earth Charter Initiative" is a global network that promotes and implements the values and principles of the Earth Charter.
- **mindfulgreen @mindfulgreen**.
- **Earthjustice @Earthjustice**. Because the earth needs a good lawyer.

Bibliography

Altman, Nathanial. *The Deva Handbook: How to Work with Nature's Subtle Energies.* Rochester, VT: Destiny, 1995.

Army, U.S. Department of the. *The Illustrated Guide to Edible Wild Plants.* Miami, FL: BN, 2009.

Awiakta, Marilou. *Selu: Seeking the Corn-Mother's Wisdom.* Golden, CO: Fulcrum, 1993.

Bailey, Liberty Hyde. *The Holy Earth: Toward a New Environmental Ethic.* Mineola, NY: Dover Publications Inc., 2009.

Barnes, Henry. *A Life for the Spirit: Rudolf Steiner in the Crosscurrents of Our Time.* Great Barrington, MA: SteinerBooks, 1997.

Bellwood, Peter. *First Farmers: The Origins of Agricultural Societies.* Hoboken, NJ:
Wiley-Blackwell, 2004.

Berry, Thomas. *The Dream of the Earth.* San Francisco, CA: Sierra Club Books, 1988.

——. *Evening Thoughts: Reflecting on Earth as Sacred Community.* San Francisco, CA: Sierra Club Books, 2006.

——. *The Great Work: Our Way into the Future.* New York: Broadway, 2000.

Berry, Wendell, and Norman Wirzba. *The Art of the Commonplace: The Agrarian Essays of Wendell Berry.* Berkeley, CA: Counterpoint, 2003.

——., and Pollan, Michael. *Bringing it to the Table: On Farming and Food.* Berkeley, CA: Counterpoint, 2009.

——. *The Unsettling of America: Culture & Agriculture.* San Francisco: Sierra Club Books, 1977.

Brown, Lester R. *World on the Edge: How to Prevent Environmental and Economic Collapse*. New York: W.W. Norton & Co., 2011.

Brown, Peter G., and Geoffrey Garver. *Right Relationship: Building a Whole Earth Economy.* San Francisco, CA: Berrett-Koehler Publishers, 2009.

Burns, Deborah, ed., et al. *The Xerces Society Guide: Attracting Native Pollinators: Protecting North America's Bees and Butterflies*. North Adams, MA: Storey, 2011.

Callahan, Phillip S. *Tuning In to Nature: Infrared Radiation and the Insect Communication System*. Greenwich, CT: Devin-Adair Publishing, 1976

Capra, Fritjof. *The Tao of Physics*. Berkeley, CA: Shambala, 1975.

Castaneda, Carlos. *Journey To Ixtlan: The Lessons of Don Juan*. New York: Simon & Schuster, 1977.

——. *The Teachings of Don Juan: A Yaqui Way of Knowledge*. New York: Ballantine, 1971.

Catches, Pete S., Sr., Peter V. Catches, ed. *Sacred Fireplace (Oceti Wakan): Life and Teachings of a Lakota Medicine Man*. Santa Fe, NM: Clear Light Publishers, 1999.

Coleby, Pat. *Natural Cattle Care*. Austin, TX: Acres U.S.A., 2010.

Coleman, Eliot. *Four-Season Harvest: Organic Vegetables From Your Home Garden All Year Long*. White River Junction, VT: Chelsea Green, 1999.

——. *The New Organic Grower: A Master's Manual of Tools and Techniques for the Home and Market Gardener*. White River Junction, VT: Chelsea Green, 1995.

——. *The Winter Harvest Handbook: Year-Round Vegetable Production Using Deep-Organic Techniques and Unheated Greenhouses*. White River Junction, VT: Chelsea Green, 2009.

Conrad, Ross. *Natural Beekeeping: Organic Approaches to Modern Apiculture*. White River Junction, VT: Chelsea Green, 2007.

Creasy, Rosalind. *The Complete Book of Edible Landscaping: Home Landscaping with Food-Bearing Plants and Resource-Saving Techniques*. San Francisco, CA: Sierra Club Books, 1982.

Cruickshank, Tom. *Living The Country Dream: Stories From Harrowsmith Country Life*. Toronto, Canada: Firefly, 2007.

Damerow, Gail. *The Backyard Homestead Guide to Raising Farm Animals*. North Adams, MA: Storey, 2011

De Dan, Rose. *Tails of a Healer: Animals, Reiki & Shamanism*. Bloomington, IN: Authorhouse, 2008.

Desy, Phylameana lila. *The Everything Reiki Book: Channel Your Positive Energy to Reduce Stress, Promote Healing, and Enhance Your Quality of Life*. Cincinnati, OH: Adams Media Corporation, 2004.

Drake, Michael. *The Shamanic Drum: A Guide to Sacred Drumming*. Mt. Angel, OR: Talking Drum Publications, 1991.

——. *I Ching: The Tao of Drumming*. Mt. Angel, OR: Talking Drum Publications, 2003.

Dyer, Wayne W. *The Power of Intention*. Carlsbad, CA: Hay House, 2004.

Eagle Feather, Ken. *A Toltec Path*. Charlottesville, VA: Hampton Roads, 1995.

——. Toltec *Dreaming: Don Juan's Teachings on the Energy Body*. Rochester, VT: Bear & Co., 2007.

Eisler, Riane. *The Chalice and the Blade: Our History, Our Future*. San Francisco, CA: HarperOne, 1988.

——. *The Real Wealth of Nations: Creating a Caring Economics*. San Francisco, CA: Berrett-Koehler, 2008.

Ewing, Jim PathFinder. *Clearing: A Guide to Liberating Energies Trapped in Buildings and Lands*. Forres, Scotland: Findhorn Press, 2006.

——. *Dreams of the Reiki Shaman: Expanding Your Healing Power*. Forres, Scotland: Findhorn Press, 2011.

———. *Finding Sanctuary in Nature: Simple Ceremonies in the Native American Tradition of Healing Yourself and Others*. Forres, Scotland: Findhorn Press, 2007.

———. *Healing Plants and Animals From a Distance: Curative Principles and Applications.* Forres, Scotland: Findhorn Press, 2007.

———. *Reiki Shamanism: A Guide to Out-of-Body Healing.* Forres, Scotland: Findhorn Press, 2008.

The Findhorn Community. *The Findhorn Garden: Pioneering a New Vision of Man and Nature in Cooperation*. New York: HarperCollins, 1976.

———. *The Findhorn Garden Story*. Forres, Scotland: Findhorn Press, 2008.

Floyd, Margaret. *Eating Naked: Unprocessed, Unpolluted & Undressed Eating for a Healthier, Sexier You*. Oakland, CA: New Harbinger, 2011.

Fukuoka, Mansanobu, et al., *The One-Straw Revolution: An Introduction to Natural Farming*. New York: New York Review of Books, 1978.

Fulton, Elizabeth, and Kathleen Prasad. *Animal Reiki: Using Energy to Heal the Animals in Your Life*. Berkeley, CA: Ulysses, 2006.

Gaia, Laurelle Shanti. *The Book On Karuna Reiki®*. Harsel, CO: Infinite Light. Healing Studies Center Inc., 2001.

Gregson, Bob, and Bonnie Gregson. *Rebirth of the Small Family Farm*. Austin, TX; Acres U.S.A., 2004.

Harner, Michael. *The Way of the Shaman*. New York: Harper, 1980.

Hartmann, Thom. *The Last Hours of Ancient Sunlight: The Fate of the World and What We Can Do Before It's Too Late*. New York: Broadway, 2004.

Hartung, Tammi. *Homegrown Herbs: A Complete Guide to Growing, Using, and Enjoying More Than 100 Herbs*. North Adams, MA: Storey, 2011.

Heinberg, Richard. *The End of Growth: Adapting to Our New Economic Reality.* Gabriola Island, BC, Canada: New Society Publishers, 2011.

Hemenway, Toby. *Gaia's Garden: A Guide To Home-Scale Permaculture, 2nd ed.* White River Junction, VT: Chelsea Green, 2009.

Hesterman, Oran B. *Fair Food: Growing a Healthy, Sustainable Food System for All.* New York: PublicAffairs, 2011.

Hopkins, Lynda. *The Wisdom of the Radish: And Other Lessons Learned on a Small Farm.* Seattle, WA: Sasquatch, 2011.

Houston, Jean and Margaret Rubin. *Manual for the Peacemaker: An Iroquois Legend to Heal Self and Society.* New York: Quest Books, 1994.

Howard, Albert. *The Soil and Health: A Study of Organic Agriculture (Culture of the Land).* Lexington, KY: The University of Kentucky Press, 2006.

Ingerman, Sandra. *Medicine for the Earth: How to Transform Personal and Environmental Toxins.* New York: Three Rivers Press, 2000.

——. *Shamanic Journeying: A Beginner's Guide.* Boulder, CO: Sounds True, 2004.

——. *Soul Retrieval: Mending the Fragmented Self.* San Francisco, CA: Harper, 1991.

——. *Welcome Home: Following Your Soul's Journey Home.* San Francisco, CA: Harper, 1993.

Jackson, Wes. *Consulting the Genius of the Place: An Ecological Approach to a new Agriculture.* Berkeley, CA: Counterpoint, 2010.

Kaplan, Rachel, and Ruby K. Blume. *Urban Homesteading: Heirloom Skills for Sustainable Living.* New York: Skyhorse, 2011.

Katz, Sandor Ellix. *Wild Fermentation: The Flavor, Nutrition, and Craft of Live-Culture Foods.* White River Junction, VT: Chelsea Green, 2003.

Kelly, Maureen J. *Reiki and the Healing Buddha.* Twin Lakes, WI: Lotus Press, 2000.

Kessler, Brad. *Goat Song: A Seasonal Life, A Short History of Herding, and the Art of Making Cheese*. New York: Scribner, 2009.

Kingsolver, Barbara, et al. *Animal, Vegetable, Miracle: A Year of Food Life*. New York: Harper, 2008.

Larkcom, Joy. *Creative Vegetable Gardening*. New York: Sterling, 2008.

Lee, Andrew W., and George DeVault, ed. *Backyard Market Gardening: The Entrepreneur's Guide to Selling What You Grow*. Buena Vista, VA: Good Earth, 1992.

LeMay, Eric. *Immortal Milk: Adventures in Cheese*. New York: Free Press, 2010.

Logsdon, Gene. *A Sanctuary of Trees: Beechnuts, Birdsongs, Baseball Bats, and Benedictions*. White River Junction, VT: Chelsea Green, 2012.

——. *Holy Sh*t: Managing Manure to Save Mankind*. White River Junction, VT: Chelsea Green, 2010.

——. *Living at Nature's Pace: Farming and the American Dream*. White River Junction, VT: Chelsea Green, 2000.

Lovel, Hugh. *A Biodynamic Farm, For Growing Wholesome Food*. Austin, TX: Acres U.S.A., 2000.

Marchese, C. Marina. *Honeybee: Lessons From An Accidental Beekeeper*. New York: Black Dog & Levanthall, 2009.

Mather, Robin. *A Garden of Unearthly Delights: Bioengineering and the Future of Food*. New York: Dutton, 1995.

——. *The Feast Nearby: How I lost my job, buried a marriage, and found my way by keeping chickens, foraging, preserving, bartering, and eating locally (all on $40 a week)*. Berkeley, CA: Ten Speed Press, 2011.

McElvaine, Robert S. *Eve's Seed: Biology, the Sexes and the Course of History*. New York: McGraw-Hill, 2000.

McFadden, Steven. *The Call of the Land: An Agrarian Primer for the 21st Century*. Nashville, TN: NorLightsPress, 2009.

——., and Trauger Groh. *Farms of Tomorrow: Community Supported Farms, Farm Supported Communities.* East Troy, WI: Biodynamic Gardening and Farming Association, 1990.

——., and Trauger Groh. *Farms of Tomorrow Revisited: Community Supported Farms, Farm Supported Communities.* East Troy, WI: Biodynamic Gardening and Farming Association, 2000.

McKibbin, Bill. *Eaarth: Making a Life on a Tough New Planet.* New York: Times Books, 2010.

McMillan, Tracie. *The American Way of Eating: Undercover at Walmart, Applebee's, Farm Fields and the Dinner Table.* New York: Scribner, 2012.

Medicine Eagle, Brooke. *The Last Ghost Dance: A Guide for Earth Mages.* New York: Wellspring/Ballantine, 2000.

——. *Buffalo Woman Comes Singing.* New York: Ballantine Books, 1991.

Melchizedek, Drunvalo. *Ancient Secrets of the Flower of Life,* vols. 1 and 2. Flagstaff, AZ: Light Technology Publishing, 1990.

Melody. *Love Is In The Earth: A Kaleidoscope of Crystals.* Wheat Ridge, CO: Earth-Love Publishing House, Ltd., 1995.

Nation, Allan. *The Moving Feast: A Cultural History of Heritage Foods in Southeast Mississippi.* Ridgeland, MS: Green Park Press, 2010.

National Audubon Society. *National Audubon Society Field Guide to North American Wildflowers—Eastern Region.* New York: Knopf, 2001.

Nearing, Scott, and Helen Nearing. *The Good Life: Helen and Scott Nearing's Sixty Years of Self-Sufficient Living.* New York: Schocken, 1989.

Nestle, Marion. *Safe Food: The Politics of Food Safety, 2nd ed.* Berkeley, CA: University of California Press, 2010.

Paglia, Camille. *Personae: Art and Decadence from Nefertiti to Emily Dickinson.* New York: Vintage Books, 1990.

Patel, Raj. *Stuffed and Starved: The Hidden Battle for the World Food System*. Brooklyn: Melville House, 2008.

Pert, Candace B., Ph.D. *Molecules of Emotion: The Science Behind Mind-Body Medicine*. New York: Simon & Schuster, 1999.

Petter, Frank Arjava. *Reiki: The Legacy of Dr. Usui*. Twin Lakes, WI: Shangri-La Press, 1998.

——., and Usui, Dr. Mikao. *The Original Reiki Handbook of Dr. Mikao Usui*. Twin Lakes, WI: Lotus Press, 1999.

Petrini, Carlo. *Slow Food Nation: Why Our Food Should Be Good, Clean and Fair*. New York: Rizzoli Ex Libris, 2007.

Pogacnik, Marko. *Nature Spirits & Elemental Beings: Working with the Intelligence in Nature*. Forres, Scotland: Findhorn Press, 2011.

Pollan, Michael. *The Botany of Desire: A Plant's-Eye View of the World*. New York: Random House, 2002.

——. *In Defense of Food: An Eater's Manifesto*. New York: Penguin, 2009.

——. *The Omnivore's Dilemma: A Natural History of Four Meals*. New York: Penguin, 2007.

——. *Second Nature: A Gardener's Education*. New York: Grove Press, 2003.

Quinn, Daniel. *Ishmael: An Adventure of the Mind and Spirit*. New York: Bantam, 1995.

Rand, William Lee. *Reiki: The Healing Touch: First and Second Degree Manual*.

Southfield, MI: Vision Publications, 1991.

Ransome, Hilda M. *The Sacred Bee in Ancient Times and Folklore*. New York: Dover, 2004.

Redmond, Layne. *When the Drummers Were Women: A Spiritual History of Rhythm*.

New York: Three Rivers Press 1997.

Revkin, Andrew. *Global Warming: Understanding the Forecast*. New York: Abbeville Press, 1992.

Roberts, Paul. *The End of Food*. Boston: Houghton Mifflin, 2008.

Rodale, Maria. *Organic Manifesto: How Organic Food Can Heal Our Planet, Feed the World, and Keep Us Safe*. Emmaus, PA: Rodale, 2011.

Rushing, Felder. *Slow Gardening: A No-Stress Philosophy for All Senses and Seasons*. White River Junction, VT: Chelsea Green, 2011.

Salatin, Joel. *The Sheer Ecstasy of Being a Lunatic Farmer*. Swoope, VA: Polyface, 2010.

———. *You Can Farm: The Entrepreneur's Guide to Start and Succeed in a Farming Enterprise*. Swoope, VA: Polyface, 1998.

Sheldrake, Rupert. *Morphic Resonance: The Nature of Formative Causation*. South Paris, ME: Park Creek Press, 2009.

Spiegelman, Annie. *Talking Dirt: The Dirt Diva's Down-to-Earth Guide to Organic Gardening*. New York: Perigee, 2010.

Stark, Tim. *Heirloom: Notes from an Accidental Tomato Farmer*. New York: Broadway, 2009.

Steiner, Rudolf, et al. *Agriculture*. Junction City, OR: Bio-Dynamic Farming and Gardening Association, 1993.

———., and Thomas Braatz. *Bees*. Great Barrington, MA: SteinerBooks, 1998.

———., and Hugh J. Courtney. *What is Biodynamics? A Way to Heal and Revitalize the Earth: Seven Lectures*. Great Barrington, MA: SteinerBooks, 2005.

Stewart, Amy. *The Earth Moved*. Chapel Hill, NC: Algonquin Books of Chapel Hill, 2004.

Stoll, Steven. *Larding the Lean Earth: Soil and Society in Nineteenth-Century America*. New York: Hill & Wang, 2002.

Swerdlow, Joel L., ed. *Nature's Medicine: Plants That Heal*. Washington, D.C.: National Geographic Society, 2000.

Symonds, George W., and A. W. Merwin. *The Shrub Identification Book: The Visual Method for the Practical Identification of Shrubs,*

Including Woody Vines and Ground Covers. New York: William Morrow, 1973.

Thun, Maria, and Mattias K. Thun. *The North American Biodynamic Sowing and Planting Calendar, 2011*. Edinburgh, Scotland: Floris, 2010.

Tyndale, John. *Heat Considered as a Mode of Motion*. Boston, MA: Adamant Media Corporation, 2001.

Walters, Charles. *Eco-Farm: An Acres U.S.A. Primer*. Austin, TX: Acres U.S.A., 2003.

——. *Weeds: Control Without Poisons*. Austin, TX: Acres U.S.A., 1999.

Warren, Karen J., and Duane L. Cady. *Bringing Peace Home: Feminism, Violence, and Nature*. Bloomington, IN: University of Indiana Press, 1996.

Watson, James. *DNA: The Secret of Life*. New York: Alfred A Knopf, 2003.

Weaver, Sue. *The Backyard Goat: An Introductory Guide to Keeping Productive Pet Goats*. North Adams, MA: Storey, 2011.

Weber, Carl, ed. *Food Inc.: A Participant Guide: How Industrial Food is Making Us Sicker, Fatter, and Poorer – And What You Can Do About It*. New York: PublicAffairs, 2009.

Welch, Bryan. *Beautiful and Abundant: Building the World We Want*. Lawrence, KS: B&A Books, 2010.

Wilkinson, Renee. *Modern Homestead: Grow, Raise, Create*. New York: Fulcrum, 2011.

Wirzba, Norman. *Food & Faith: A Theology of Eating*. New York: Cambridge University Press, 2011.

Ywahoo, Dhyani. *Voices of the Ancestors: Cherokee Teachings from the Wisdom Fire*. Boston, MA: Shambhala Publications, 1987.

Zukov, Gary. *The Dancing Wu Li Masters: An Overview of the New Physics*. New York: William Morrow, 1979.

Endnotes

INTRODUCTION

1. PathFinder's PathWays are the author's popular meditations/observations that have been reprinted in newspapers, magazines, and websites all over the world. They are designed to allow a broadening of understanding and perspective that at the same time raises one's vibration rate. Since they were begun as "Ascension Tests" in 2002, they have been included in each of the author's newsletters, *Keeping In Touch*, that has subscribers across the United States and 28 foreign countries and on his website, Healing The Earth/Ourselves, *www.blueskywaters.com*.

CHAPTER 1

1. For more, see: *Agriculture* by Rudolf Steiner, translated from the German (Bio-Dynamic Farming and Gardening Association, 1993).

2. For an excellent treatment of the many ways in which the clash of cultures between Native Americans and Europeans both benefited and resulted in a loss for society (with good pointers for the future), see Jean Houston and Margaret Rubin's *Manual for the Peacemaker: An Iroquois Legend to Heal Self and Society* (Quest Books, 1994). The Iroquois are cited because of the extensive literature regarding them, from first contact in the 1600s through the 18th century; most of the accounts of relations between indigenous peoples and Europeans in America and later are colored by territorial ambitions or outright prejudice. Among the interesting observations regarding early Iro-

quois contact, which can be inferred among other matrilineal tribes in America, is the fact that women as property owners enjoyed tremendous power and freedom within the tribes. Their status was higher than in European culture, their wealth immeasurably greater, and indigenous peoples ate better with a wider and healthier variety of foods than Europeans (which, along with the hygienic practice of daily bathing, which was not followed by Europeans, gave a higher quality of life). The lands indigenous peoples settled were generally better than the choices of early colonies, as well. Many of the early accounts of European women being "kidnapped by savages" were, in fact, women left abandoned to their fates in European culture with the death of—or abuse by—a spouse leaving for the safety and better living conditions of Native life.

3. For a telling treatment of humankind's shift from "leavers," or indigenous ways of respect for the soil, Earth and all beings, to "takers," or exploiters of Earth and a throwaway society, see Daniel Quinn's *Ishmael: An Adventure of the Mind and Spirit* (Bantam, 1995). For broader treatments of "The Fall," see Norman Wirzba's outstanding *Food & Faith: A Theology of Eating* (Cambridge University Press, 2011).

4. *The Nag Hammadi Library* by James M. Robinson, et al. Revised Edition. New York: HarperSanFrancisco, 1990.

5. *The Gospel of the Essenes: The Unknown Books of the Essenes & Lost Scrolls of the Essene Brotherhood* by Edmond Bordeaux. Essex, England: The C.W. Daniel Co. Ltd., 1974.

6. See *The Infancy Gospels of James and Thomas: The Scholars Bible* by Ronald F. Hock, (Polebridge Press, 1995), also Hock's *The Life of Mary and the Birth of Jesus: The Ancient Infancy Gospel of James* (Ulysses Press, 1997).

CHAPTER 2

1. "Thomas Jefferson's Legacy in Gardening and Food" by Peter Hatch, *Huffington Post*, Sept. 13, 2010.

2. "Organic Can Feed The World" by Barry Estabrook, *The Atlantic*, Dec. 5, 2011.

CHAPTER 3

1. Richard Heinberg sees developing stronger local, intentional communities as a viable strategy for the future in his book *The End of Growth: Adapting to Our New Economic Reality* (New Society Publishers, 2011). The need for similar strategies is urgently made in Lester R. Brown's *World on the Edge: How to Prevent Environmental and Economic Collapse* (W.W. Norton & Co., 2011).

    For more information, see: The Global Ecovillage Network (GEN). It is a growing network of sustainable communities and initiatives that bridge different cultures, countries, and continents. GEN serves as an umbrella organization for ecovillages, transition town initiatives, intentional communities, and ecologically minded individuals worldwide. Website: *http://gen. ecovillage.org*

    Also, see: The Fellowship For Intentional Community. It includes ecovillages, cohousing communities, residential land trusts, communes, student co-ops, urban housing cooperatives, intentional living, alternative communities, cooperative living, and other projects where people strive together with a common vision. Website: *http://www.ic.org/*

2. The human capacity for peace, ahimsa, or Sanskrit "noninjury." the ethical principle of not causing harm to other living things, found in Jainism, Hinduism, and Buddhism, is a powerful approach toward food. Organizations around the world have em-

braced the concept of nonviolence in approaching ideas, incorporating *ahimsa* as a guiding principle. This offers avenues for a new approach toward food, not only in the avoidance of harm to animals *as* food but avoiding as much harm as possible to plants, animals, ecosystems, and Earth in the *production* of food. Yoga (from the Sanskrit word for "union"), an Indian Hindu spiritual practice founded in India that has seen an explosion of growth globally in the past decade, can be a powerful medium of promoting food consciousness and spiritual eating.

In traditional Hinduism, the practice of yoga involves inner contemplation, including both meditation practice and ethics, a fact often obscured by the modern focus on physical health, fitness, and flexibility. Indeed, when looking at the *Yoga Sutras*, fundamental yoga principles compiled by Patanjali (believed to have lived in the 1st century BCE), the yoga postures (*asana*) are the third limb of the Eight Limb Path (Ashtanga Yoga). The first limb is *yama*, or moral code, which includes *ahimsa*, as well as *satya*, a principle of truthfulness, which is all too lacking when it comes to food production. Greater integrity is indeed a quality that needs promoting when it comes to our food, especially regarding additives and nonfood "food products." The second limb of *niyama*, or personal discipline, can help guide our own behaviors—in the principles of purity, contentment, endurance, self-study, and dedication—but also in requiring high moral and ethical practices by those who produce our food. By applying the full range of yoga principles to food and eating, we each can help transform our world.

3. Seed-saving and nurturing of heritage seeds is essential to maintain biodiversity of the planet.

   Some resources:

   Article – How to create a seed lending library: Richmond Grows Seed Lending Libary: *www.richmondgrows.org/create-a-library. html*

   Some seed libraries:

   - BASIL (Bay Area Seed Interchange Library) - Berkeley, California, www.ecologycenter.org/BASIL
   - Hudson Valley Seed Library - Accord, New York - www. seedlibrary.org
   - Native Seeds SEARCH - Tucson, Arizona. - www.native-seeds.org
   - Richmond Grows Seed Lending Library - Richmond, California, www.richmondgrows.org
   - SLoLA - Seed Library of Los Angeles - Los Angeles, California, www.slola.org
   - Westcliffe Seed Lending Library - Westcliffe, Colorado, www.westcliffegrows.weebly.com
   - Seed Savers Exchange, (319) 382-5990; Decorah, Iowa.
   - SeedLiving Exchange: www.seedliving.ca.

   Some organic, heirloom, and heritage seed companies:

   - Baker Creek Heirloom Seeds, (417) 924-8917; Mansfield, Missouri.
   - Johnny's Selected Seeds, 1-800-854-2580; Winslow, Maine.
   - Peaceful Valley Farm Supply, (888) 784-1722; Grass Valley, California.
   - Seeds of Change, (888) 762-7333; Santa Fe, New Mexico.
   - Southern Exposure Seed Exchange, (540) 894-9480; Mineral, Virginia.

About the Author

Jim PathFinder Ewing (Nvnehi Awatisgi) is a Reiki Master teacher, journalist, and author who also teaches Reiki Shamanism. For more, see his website: *www.blueskywaters.com*, or follow him on Facebook, *http://www.facebook.com/pages/Jim-PathFinder-Ewing/19604582873*, or on Twitter *@edibleprayers*.

FINDHORN PRESS

Life-Changing Books

For a complete catalogue,
please contact:

Findhorn Press Ltd
117-121 High Street,
Forres IV36 1AB,
Scotland, UK

t +44 (0)1309 690582
f +44 (0)131 777 2711
e info@findhornpress.com

or consult our catalogue online
(with secure order facility) on
www.findhornpress.com

For information on the Findhorn Foundation:
www.findhorn.org

Further Jim PathFinder Ewing titles

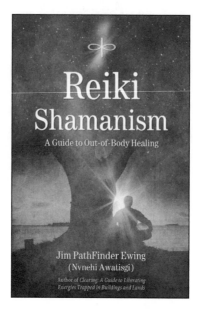

Reiki Shamanism

Learn how to heal people, places, and things, whether at hand or from a distance. Presented by an expert in both traditions, the techniques of Reiki and the principles of shamanism are explained in simple, concise terms, then brought together using real-life examples to show how Reiki can be practiced within the shamanic journey. Supported by mastery exercises, references to other books, and internet resources, both novices and experienced practitioners will expand their knowledge and ability to help subjects clear old energies and accelerate their "soul purpose."

978-1-84409-133-1

Further Jim PathFinder Ewing titles

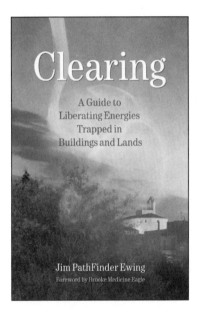

Clearing

Working from the premise that every natural and human-made space has an energy of its own that can physically and emotionally affect anyone in that space, this introduction to ancient practices of environmental shamanism - or transformation of the energy of spaces - explains in practical terms how to liberate old, unproductive energy that may be stored in any space, making room for new vibrations to circulate and increase inhabitants well-being. Real-life examples, guided exercises, annotated endnotes, and an extensive glossary to supplement case studies are also included.

978-1-84409-082-2

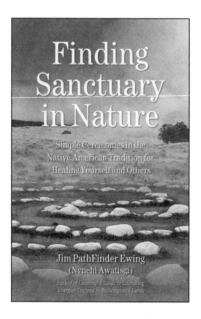

Finding Sanctuary in Nature

*Included are hands-on exercises, step-by-step instructions for cer-
emonies, and notebook items from the author's own life. Finding
Sanctuary in Nature takes Clearing, the author's first book, to the
next level - from clearing spaces of unwanted energies to creating
sacred spaces within which to perform simple ceremonies for healing oneself and others. The reader will learn how to: Connect with
spirit guides and angels · Interpret symbols · Create ceremonies for
daily living · Heal the Earth and much more…*

978-1-84409-095-2

Further Jim PathFinder Ewing titles

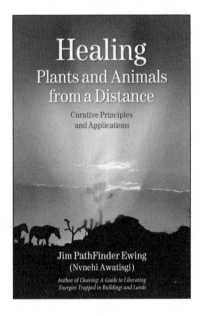

Healing Plants and Animals from a Distance

*Become conscious of your healing abilities using simple rituals,
whose roots draw from shamanism, spirituality, religion, Native
American studies, vibrational energy, and alternative medicine.
This manual demonstrates not only how to gain the knowledge and
wisdom afforded by various spirit beings, guides, and helpers,
but also how to apply this knowledge in the natural world.
Visualization, prayer, and other techniques for accessing the vibration rates and consciousness of living things are also explored.*

978-1-84409-111-9

green press
INITIATIVE

MIX
Paper from responsible sources

FSC
www.fsc.org

FSC® C013483